HANNAH WEINER'S OPEN HOUSE

Hannah Weiner

edited and with an introduction by
Patrick F. Durgin

Published by Kenning Editions
www.kenningeditions.com

ISBN: 0-9767364-1-1
ISBN13: 978-0-9767364-1-7

Order from Small Press Distribution
1341 Seventh Street, Berkeley CA 94710
www.spdbooks.org
1-800-869-7553

The publication of this book has been made possible, in part, by the generosity
of the following donors to Kenning Editions: Charles Bernstein, Susan Schultz,
Lyn Hejinian, Marcia Hofer, Marcia Pevsner, David Pavelich, Adalaide Morris,
Barbara Guest, Kevin Killian, Norma Cole, Pierre Joris, Alan Golding, Liz Kotz,
Barett Watten, Hank Lazer, and Andrea Troolin.

Cover design by Quemadura.
www.quemadura.net

HANNAH WEINER'S OPEN HOUSE

SATURDAY, OCTOBER 4

1--3PM   Vito Acconci, 102 Christopher Street

3PM   Bernadette Mayer; Bernadette Mayer has no home.
                   She will be on the North East
                   corner of Christopher and Hudson
                   Street

3--5PM   John Perreault, 242 West 10th Street

5--7PM   Hannah Weiner, 36 West 26th Street

SUNDAY, OCTOBER 5

1--3PM   Abraham Lubelski, 109 Spring Street

3--5PM   Marjorie Strider, 113 Greene Street

5--7PM   Arakawa, 124 West Houston Street

CONTENTS

INTRODUCTION

Hannah Weiner's influence extends from the sixties New York avant-garde, where she was part of an unprecedented confluence of poets, performance and visual artists including David Antin, Scott Burton, Phillip Glass, Meredith Monk, John Perreault, Carolee Schneeman, and Andy Warhol. Like fellow traveler Jackson Mac Low, she became an important part of the L=A=N=G=U=A=G=E movement of the 1970s and '80s, and her influence can be seen today in the so-called "New Narrative" work stemming from the San Francisco Bay Area. Her most impressive work, *Clairvoyant Journal*, was begun in the early '70s and published in excerpt by Angel Hair (edited by Anne Waldman and Lewis Warsh and typeset by Barrett Watten) in 1978. The entire *Clairvoyant Journal* project, beginning with *The Fast* (United Artists, 1992) and *Country Girl* (Kenning Editions, 2004), and continuing with *Pictures and Early Words*, *Big Words*, and the *Clairvoyant Journal* proper, spans a period synonymous with the onset of what was diagnosed as psychotic episodes indicative of schizophrenia. All but *The Fast* have long been out of print, but were published online as high resolution scans of the original manuscripts by the University of California at San Diego's Archive for New Poetry as *The Early and Clairvoyant Journals* in 2004. Along with substantial online editions of works ranging from Weiner's first chapbook of poetry, *Magritte Poems* (Poetry Newsletter, 1970), and obscure contributions to little magazines of the so-called mimeograph revolution, such as "Sign Language of the American Indian," to the notorious recordings of the *Clairvoyant Journal*, several of her works remain available in their original editions, including an early "clairvoyantly written" poem, *Nijole's House* (Potes & Poets, 1981, rpt. 2004) and the posthumous long sequence *Page* (Roof, 2002). (Interested readers are encouraged to visit Weiner's author page at the Electronic Poetry Center: epc.buffalo.edu/authors/weiner.) With other posthumous publications of late, her work continues to be discussed, in surely too small a measure, by scholars in feminist studies, poetics, and, very recently, disability studies. But there does not yet exist a representative selection spanning her decades of poetic output. *Hannah Weiner's Open House* aims to remedy this with previously uncollected or never-before-published work, including performance texts, early New York School influenced lyric poems, odes and remembrances to/of Mac Low and Ted Berrigan, and later "clair-style" works. The book constitutes a "selected works," setting the most readily publishable materials from her archives alongside passages with which some readers may be familiar. What I hope to represent with this selection is the invigorating variety of forms and methods Weiner employed, of which most were entirely original creations. By doing so, the book may clarify her place within one of the most compelling traditions of recent USAmerican poetics: radical modernist literary experimentation as social ethics.

Weiner was born in Providence, Rhode Island in 1928, graduated from Classical High School, and, in 1950, from Radcliffe College. Near the end of a notable career as a lingerie designer in New York City, she began giving performances, including "Hannah Weiner at Her Job," "World Works" and "Street Works." The latter were documented in the avant-garde journal edited by Vito Acconci and Bernadette Mayer, *0-9*. The complete run of *0-9* (published in 2006 by Ugly Duckling Presse) contains roughly contemporary accounts of these projects, whereas those included here were composed later, probably in the mid-1980s, and are somewhat more comprehensive. And although Weiner studied poetry with Bill Berkson and Kenneth Koch at the New School for Social Research in 1963, the major thrust of her work of this period culminated in further intermedia performances, documented in her second major book of poetry, *Code Poems* (Open Book, 1982), to which Sol Lewit contributed blurb. As Mac Low and Redell Olsen have written, Weiner's concern was with forging a poetics of translation. Not between languages, nor necessarily between media, but the onus was on the poet to instigate an event of phenomenologically complex realism. In this sense, one can draw a clear trajectory from the *Magritte Poems* to the last works, where language and consciousness come under meticulous scrutiny in the context of inter- and intra-personal relations. Perhaps most notable is the depth with which Weiner charted the continuum between persons and cultures, with the "page" or "large-sheet" of poetry figured as a socio-political field. Although the literary-historical record has yet to significantly acknowledge the fact, Weiner's efforts in this direction sound a unique take on the larger "New American" project of composition by field, and can be usefully contextualized in a lineage stemming from Gertrude Stein's radical portraiture (as dear to Robert Duncan as to John Ashbery). And like Gertrude Stein's most important works, Weiner's work is playful, at times opaque and baffling, but strangely and thus importantly familiar.

Although I knew I couldn't feasibly present a "collected works," in editing *Hannah Weiner's Open House*, I attempted to present an adequate sense of the narrative arc of Weiner's development as a writer. A manageable array of works, with new as well as old readers in mind, had to run only roughly chronologically. A substantial amount of her archival material is difficult to date exactly. Moreover, Weiner worked in various forms simultaneously, not to mention the fact that her books appeared often out of sync with the major developments of her "career." We begin with the book's namesake, an invitation found among Weiner's papers in the Archive for New Poetry. Happenings such as this were inherently collaborative affairs, blurring the lines of authorship between artist, interpreter, and audience. The "Street Works" project of spring 1969 was a loosely-knit carnival of the new conceptual/intermedia/performance scene that was to provide a crucial venue for the previous year's debut of the *Code Poem* performances, which took place in New York's Central Park. It's hard to miss but essential to note the alternately whimsical and sinister valences of the transcriptions from the ostensibly universal language of the "International Code of Signals for the Use of All Nations." This "Code of Signals" is an early example of modernist stabs at universality by way of attrition, impossible attempts to drain a language of connotation and which rely on notions of native, linguistic competence. The *Code Poems* join a line of transgressive reappropriations. Writing of Louis Zukofsky and of Jackson Mac Low's respective poems using I. A. Richards and C. K. Ogden's attempt at a BASIC English word list, Barrett Watten notes that such reappropriations insist "on the constructed nature not only of subjectivity but of community... Such language, rather than assuming an inaccessible interiority, is separated from the expressivist core or poetic form as it interprets its outside sources as equally available to anyone." Clearly this is what lends works such as "Any Chance of War?" their peculiar powers to amuse and incite.

As Weiner's scrutiny resolved itself into self-scrutiny, first via odes and letters to close friends such as Ted Berrigan, Bernadette Mayer, and Mac Low, among others, then via the narrative of her extraordinary experience of psychic disturbances in the *Early and Clairvoyant Journals*, it extended to those indelible but tenaciously unstable identity categories of nativity prevalent in her late works. Hence her negotiation of gender questions, high-low cultural emissions (from the museum wall to network television news, the "Strider" poems to the newly reprinted *Weeks*), and her unique and problematic engagement with the American Indian Movement. By 1984's *Spoke*, her most anthologized work, these concerns had converged in a form beginning to resemble, after the page-wide, tri-vocal *Clairvoyant Journal*, something like a new, highly paratactic and quasi-concrete lyric. But the apostrophic, lyric address of these works constitutes disruption, rather than an authoritative or narratalogical anchor. The irony of this reversal of lyric apostrophe is not a postmodern endgame of despair, as some readings of high modernist and postmodernist poetics often insist. As Bernstein and others have remarked, Weiner's "voice," as such, actually partakes of a kind of heroism, especially when read in light of her often debilitating medical or psychic condition. Our heroine traverses semiotic collisions, such as that which provides the enabling conflict of *The Zero One*, which dramatizes the very mundane interpenetrating demands of phenomenal and epistemic zones we perhaps arrogantly employ in the interest of clarity. Translation becomes transposition in this and in related works, especially "Radcliffe and Guatemalan Women" and "Meaning Bus Halifax to Queensbury," where language from separate discourse registers produces surprising and evocative flashes of recognition.

As Judith Goldman and others have duly noted, it is disingenuous to equate what Weiner called "clairvoyance" with either illness or a supernatural gift of fortune-telling. Although Weiner's claims regarding clairvoyance are, to many readers, her calling card, it's important to relativize those claims in terms of form and content, especially form. This is why clairvoyance can be more appropriately synonymous with, in her own words, "clair-style." The development of this "style" is both described and narrated in the *Early and Clairvoyant Journals*. A concise, previously unpublished take on the phenomenal aspects of clairvoyance is provided in "The words in CAPITALS..." below. And indeed, this form is inseparable from her experience of extraordinary psychic phenomena. One year prior to the publication of the Angel Hair edition of *Clairvoyant Journal*, New Wilderness Audiographics released the now iconic recording of the March-April sections of the work, performed by Weiner with Sharon Mattlin, Margaret (Peggy) De Coursey, and Regina Beck. The cassette's liner notes offer one of the most concise and accessible synopses of the basic gambits involved. Thus it deserves quoting at length.

In 1970 Hannah Weiner began to see pictures and energy fields. Two years later she began to see words. This came after a period of intense artistic activity in the late 60s, and after experimentation with altered states of consciousness and the development of a strong belief in yoga. She was interested in signaling, and had just completed a series of Code Poem performances, using the "International Code of Signals for the Use of All Nations."

After nine months of seeing disorganized words in small print, all over the place—on curtains, walls, toes—she went on a retreat conducted by Swami Satchitananda. There, for the first time she saw words clearly printed, in capitals, on her forehead. In her typography:

$$\text{the}$$
$$\begin{matrix} & \text{n} & & \text{a} \\ \end{matrix}$$
I SEE words on my forehead, in the air$\quad$i$\quad$i
$$\text{r}$$

on other people, on the typewriter, O N T H E P A G E

These appear in the text in CAPITALS OR S P A C E D O U T

or in underlines.

At first the words appeared one at a time. Later, phrases and whole sentences began to appear, in various print sizes and in script. The words have a memory, relate to specific situations, give information not "consciously" available, answer questions, play language games, joke and tease. Sometimes she hears voices as well as seeing words.

Although the words are most often silent, Weiner started referring to them as "voices" when a second "personality" joined the original flow of words after her first retreat. The first voice often gives advice and is sometimes precognitive. The second voice is ironic. It's a telepathic receptor of thoughts from a community of mutually dedicated friends linked through empathy—a group mind.

The voices are recorded in Hannah Weiner's Clairvoyant Journals. In the 1974 Journal, lower case is used for Weiner's own voice, capitals for the first, advisor voice, which appears on her forehead, and underlines for the second voice.

The page or "large sheet" is the nexus of a painterly site of inscription, as Weiner explains in an interview, over a decade later, with Charles Bernstein, published in *The Line in Postmodern Poetry*. Her most sustained and comprehensive metacritical discussion of the ramifications of clair-style poetry, instigated in correspondence with Andrew Schelling and published in the small-press magazine *Jimmy and Lucy's House of K*, is called "Mostly about the Sentence" (1986). The prose/verse dichotomy with which most poetry readers are quite taken is definitively dissolved in the "group mind" of what Weiner later called "silent teaching."

Apparently one of the earliest iterations of this novel form of communication is Weiner's "clairvoyantly written" ode to her friend and colleague, "Jackson Mac Low." He is "impossible as a leader," despite the entreaty to "experiment in any form that occurs to [J]ackson." The figure of Mac Low, obviously an estimable one in the New York avant-garde of the late twentieth century, is neither truly an "obtrusion" or "complete line," nor a facet of hallucinatory symptomology. The poem's remarkable air of compassion could hardly survive either. A description for a poetry workshop Weiner apparently never had the opportunity to formally teach, entitled "Awareness and Communication" and published in an issue of the journal *Kiosk*, indicates that achieving this air of compassion is neither Weiner's special provenance nor less than synonymous with the basic ambition of speech acts to bridge absence, whether of a being or of information.

Exploring the things that keep us from communication. A sharing of experience often leads to increased awareness. ... An assignment for any student absent from class: for the period he should be in class, to be aware of what he is doing and to think of class also – to discuss his feelings and experience at the next class. This always brings out valuable information.

It is also important to note that the poem "Jackson Mac Low" was written using margins that emulate verse margins, recalling the generic stipulations of the ode, while entirely avoiding lyric apostrophe. Formally, it serves as a bridge between the somewhat prosaic "large-sheet" lines of the earlytomid-1970s and her last major work, a sequence of verse wherein Weiner, as "sis," addresses herself incessantly, and a book thematically centered on the death of her mother, *Page* (only one page of which was marked as clairvoyantly written). One of Weiner's last published works, 1997's "Silent History," is from the "Procedures" issue of the journal *Chain*, whose contributions are variously haunted by Mac Low's mastery of procedural compositional methods. If "hear[ing]" Mac Low in oneself is a function of the silent teaching to which Weiner pays tribute, one can only imagine this early, traditional, yet clairvoyant poem stands in relation to "Silent History" as Mac Low's rather thorough descriptions of his compositional methods and performance instructions stand in relation to the poems they always accompanied. And if "Jackson Mac Low," like "Day 52," can be considered a sort of radical modernist ode, rather than a Stein-inspired "portrait," it is to Weiner's oeuvre what "Sonnet of My Death" is to Mac Low's: an occasional poem whose only event is itself. Weiner died in 1997.

Aside from inevitable omissions, particular inclusions and settings of the works in *Hannah Weiner's Open House* deserve a brief explanation. Since the page as a compositional field, and often performance or "event" score, is so crucial to the study and enjoyment of Weiner's work, I chose to scan and reprint typesettings of the works the author had the opportunity to approve in proofs, rather than resetting them for consistency of design. I have tried to respect the notion of the page as a visual field to the largest degree possible. This very impulse manifested itself differently in the case of my other major editorial project involving Weiner's *Early and Clairvoyant Journals*, where the manuscript pages were presented as the author left them to posterity, and which I discuss at length in my critical introduction to the publication. Here I reprint Watten's rendition for the Angel Hair edition of *Clairvoyant Journal* because, as Weiner herself clearly recognized, they are both beautiful and more legibly accomplished in that context. However, I have reset a few selections (such as *Magritte Poems*, *Code Poems*, and those from *Silent Teachers/ Remembered Sequel* and *We Speak Silent*) when it was feasible to produce identical settings with comparable but uniform typefaces. Furthermore, as even a brief glimpse at Weiner's archives denotes, the typewriter (and in rare cases, word processor) was a veritable collaborator in the event of composition of the "clair-style" works. So I have opted for a typeface that emulates without imitating the typewriter.

This volume has directly and indirectly benefited from the aid of many interested individuals. Charles Bernstein, the executor of Weiner's estate, has encouraged my study of Weiner's work for years and provided me complete freedom to work with and publish her archival materials. Additionally, Michael Basinski and Susan Bee provided access to some of the materials included here. I learned a great deal from conversations with those who knew the author, including Bernstein, Jerome and Diane Rothenberg, Jena Osman, Laynie Brown, Lee Ann Brown, Bernadette Mayer, Barbara Rosenthal, Lewis Warsh, Jackson Mac Low, Andrew Levy, Barrett Watten, and Lyn Hejinian. A good deal of brilliant critical writing on or involving Weiner's work has guided my work, including essays by Bernstein, Maria Damon, Thom Donovan, Mark DuCharme, Judith Goldman, Kaplan Harris, and Ron Silliman. In early 2006, Laura Elrick and Rodrigo Toscano performed "Romeo and Juliet" from the *Code Poems* as part of a fundraising event for this project, and they deserve thanks for their provocative interpretation of the poem. My typesetting and design of the interior of this book have been guided by the infallible suggestions of Jeff Clark, without whom a viable trade paperback edition of this volume might never have come to be. For sustaining me through the editing of the book, Andrea Troolin deserves special mention; the project's been developing for years, and she's always been there with support and encouragement. Adalaide Morris, my mentor and friend years ago surprised me with the gift of a copy of Weiner's *Spoke*, which is where my interest in the project truly began. I must also, finally, announce my gratitude to Weiner herself, whom I never had the opportunity to meet, but whose works have inalterably set many of my most fruitful investigations into radical modernist poetics in the right direction.

—Patrick F. Durgin
12.2.2006

Bernstein, Charles. "Hannah Weiner." *Jacket* 12 (2000). jacketmagazine.com/12/wein-bern.html

Damon, Maria. "Hannah Weiner Beside Herself: Clairvoyance After Shock or The Nice Jewish Girl Who Knew Too Much." *East Village Web.* 5 March 2004. http://www.fauxpress.com/t8/damon/p3.html.

DuCharme, Mark. "Consciousness & Contradiction: Hannah Weiner's *silent teachers/remembered sequel.*" *6ix* 5 (1997). 4-9.

Goldman, Judith. "Hannah=hannaH: Politics, Ethics, and Clairvoyance in the Work of Hannah Weiner" *differences: A Journal of Feminist Cultural Studies*, Summer 2001 v12 i2 p121

Mac Low, Jackson. "Persia/Sixteen/Code Poems." *Poetics Journal* 4 (1982): 88-97.

-----. "Sonnet of My Death." *Representative Works: 1938-1985.* New York: Roof Books, 1986: 42.

Olsen, Redell. "'Simultaneous Equivalents': Adrian Piper, Bernadette Mayer, Hannah Weiner in *0-9.*" *Performance Research* (Summer 2002): 60-65.

Watten, Barrett. "New Meaning and Poetic Vocabulary: From Coleridge to Jackson Mac Low." *The Constructivist Moment: from Material Text to Cultural Poetics.* Middletown, CT: Wesleyan University Press, 2003: 1-44.

Weiner, Hannah. "AWARENESS AND COMMUNICATION." *Kiosk* 2 (2003): 245..

-----. *Clairvoyant Journal.* Perf. Sharon Mattlin, Peggy De Coursey, Regina Beck and Hannah Weiner. Audiocassette. New Wilderness Audiographics, 1978.

Weiner, Hannah and Charles Bernstein. "Excerpts from an Interview with Hannah Weiner." *The Line in Postmodern Poetry.* Robert Frank and Henry Sayre ed. Urbana: University of Illinois Press, 1988: 187-188.

HANNAH WEINER'S OPEN HOUSE

GAIN GROUND PRESENTS

HANNAH WEINER AT HER JOB

A. H. Schreiber Co., Inc. 10 West 33 St., N.Y.C. Room 1200
Wednesdays, March 11, 18, 25   5:30-8 P.M.

Miss Weiner explains her show as follows:

"My life is my art. I am my object, a product of the process of self-awareness. I work part-time as a designer of ladies underwear to help support myself. I like my job, and the firm I work for. They make and sell a product without unnecessary competition. The people in the firm are friendly and fun to work with. The bikini pants I make sell for 49¢ and $1.00. If things can't be free, they should be as cheap as possible. Why waste time and energy to make expensive products that you waste time and energy to afford?

Art is live people. Self respect is a job if you need it. On 3 Wednesday evenings I will be at my studio, where I work. My boss, Simeon Schreiber, will be with me. There will be bikini underpants for sale, at the usual prices, and one made especially for this show by August Fabrics and A. H. Schreiber, to whom I am grateful."

Hannah Weiner is one of the co-ordinators of Street Works and World Works with John Perreault and Marjorie Strider. Her Code Poem Events were given at Spring Gallery '68 and Central Park. She co-authored the Fashion Show Poetry Event with Eduardo Costa and John Perrault, and the International Event, Summer 1969. Her performances include Theater Works at Hunter College, Spring Gallery '69 at Paula Cooper Gallery, Performance, 1970 at the Midtown Y. Her work has been shown at Dwan Gallery (Word Show II, III), The School of Visual Arts, and Gain Ground. She will participate in the "Art in the Mind" show at Oberlin College this spring. This is her first one man show.

For further information call 242-0232

WORLD WORKS

March 21, 1970 Noon

1. I wrote the word THE over WORLD WORKS
2. I vacuumed the street. The world works with a little help from us all.

I wanted to do World Works because I wanted to create the feeling that people all over the world were doing a related thing at a related time, although they would be doing it individually, without an audience and without knowledge of what others were doing. It is an act of faith. We have unknown collaborators.

I. March 15, 1969. In mid-town Manhattan, I pasted blank labels on signs, doors, walls, posts, etc. in order to draw attention to the environment.

II. April 18, 1969. I met the other Hannah Weiner. She is tall and blonde. I am short and dark. She does Psychodrama.

III. May 25, 1969. I tied up half a city block (I didn't have enough tape to tie up a whole one) with tape printed from the International Code of Signals. Decoded, the flags read: MZWT: "Secured, has, have, ing. Do not pass ahead of me." The police came 1/2 hour later and ripped down the tape.

IV. October, 1969, sponsored by the Architectural League. For the opening, Oct. 2, I hired a frankfurter wagon to give away free "wieners". This was a pun on my name. Anything or anybody can have anything or anybody's name. Hot dog wagons are everywhere part of the street environment. Unfortunately wieners (and pastrami, bologna, preserved meats) contain sodium nitrite and sodium nitrate; one a coloring agent for otherwise gray meat, one an embalming fluid. Both have a depressing effect on the mind.

     During the month of October, for IV, I did OPEN HOUSE. I invited the public into the homes of participating artists. From 3 to 26 people showed up at different places. We sat around kitchen tables, or on the floor and talked and smoked or had a party. I met new friends.

V. Dec. 21, 1969. I stood on a street corner, or in a doorway, as if I were soliciting. Women do that in that neighborhood (3rd Ave & 13 St to 3rd Ave & 14 St). It is not a nice feeling at all. I ALSO SPRINKLED STARS ON THE STREET

THE MAGRITTE POEMS

AMOROUS PERSPECTIVE

I rushed through the door.
You had bitten a way for me. (1)

MAN WITH THE NEWSPAPER (2)

1. Sat by the window
   in his wing collar.

2. Now he is gone

3. He is gone

4. Slight dominance of red velvet curtains

DANGEROUS ACQUAINTANCES

Would you rather
I turned my ass
to you? (3)
Well, say so,
don't stand there
holding a mirror.

THE CASTLE OF THE PYRENEES

Come to my summer house.
It's damp
floating over the sea,
but you can light a fire
in any French Horn.
Eagles bring you there. (4)

THE FALSE MIRROR

In your blue eye
the sky
has clouds
in it. (5)

THE ALPHABET OF REVELATIONS (6)

A key
a leaf
a stemmed pipe
a stemmed glass

twisted wire
has torn canvas
unlocked
maple dreams

the leaf also has a stem
the key also has a stem

WELL, I LAUGHED
I thought the clouds
were upside down.
They weren't.
You laughed.

Revolution! (7)

THE GOLDEN LEGEND

Magritte, damn
your stone loaves (8)
that float past
my hungry
window!

NOTES

1. See your dentist every six months for a regular check up

2. An American Paper for the American People

3. Yes

4. Sundays and Holidays. Will not run May 28, July 2, and Sept. 3

5. today and tomorrow. Precipitation probability: Tuesday 20%, Tuesday
    night and Wednesday 30%

6.

7. ¡Revolution!

8. made from wheat and rye flour, rye meal, yeast, table salt, vegetable shortening, malt, caraway seeds, caramel, onion powder, calcium propionate and water.

THE LOST EDEN OF PACO SAINZ

There is a green field
a cow
a pig
He holds a flower
She carries a bouquet
uses a feather for a sail
takes one bite from an apple.

They build houses
saddle asses in orange leather
put flowers in vases
put flowers on dresses
He sits on a horse, kills.

If he grows old,
shoots a rabbit.

Connecticut:
hills
and shadows
winding
over the
you can't see
roads
what is
behind
and leaves
many colored.

I move back
to Iowa.
It is flat
there is yellow
sunlight
and un-
interrupted
shadows
over corn
or is it
wheat
fields
where you come from.

Your flowers grow
there
almost
and
out.

The shadow is under the umbrella
the red umbrella
the green chair faces the left hand corner.

The shadow is on the right
the red and green umbrella
the yellow sand
the green chair faces three-quarter.

Under the red umbrella
by the blue sea
the green chair faces full
the shadow is round.

The shadow is under the umbrella
the red umbrella
the white sky
the green chair faces the left hand corner.

These poems and performance pieces are from the INTERNATIONAL CODE OF SIGNALS for
the Use of All Nations, British Editions 1859, 1899 and American Edition, post-war, 1931,
a visual signal system for ships at sea. Codes of signals for the use of mariners have been
published in various countries since the early 19th century. The first International Code
was drafted in 1855 by a committee set up by the British Board of Trade. Flags at that
time numbered 18, which represented the consonants of the alphabet, with the exception
of X and Z. A later version published in 1899 increased the letter flags to 26, plus an
answering pennant. Flags, one for each letter of the alphabet, are hoisted on the mast,
singly or in groups of two, three, four. Single and two flag hoists are distress signals, three
flag hoists are general signals, four flag hoists geographical signals. In addition, each flag
has a name; A, Alpha, B, Bravo, C, Charlie, etc. In combination, as CJD, "I was plundered
by a pirate," these signals comprise a complete volume of code signals. Messages can be
transmitted also by two semaphore red signal flags, and by Morse code. Visual signaling
is any method of above water communication, the transmission of which is capable of
being seen (alphabet flags, semaphore flags, Morse flashing light). Sound signaling is any
method of sending Morse signals by means of siren, whistle, foghorn, bell or other sound
apparatus. Although Morse and light signals were used in performances, only visual
signals are included (we omit radio) in this book.

THE SEMAPHORE ALPHABET

CHAR-ACTERS	HAND FLAGS	CHAR-ACTERS	HAND FLAGS	CHAR-ACTERS	HAND FLAGS	CHAR-ACTERS	HAND FLAGS
A		H		O		V	
B		I		P		W	
C ANSWER-ING SIGN		J		Q		X	
D		K		R		Y	
E		L		S		Z	
F		M		T		ATTEN-TION	
G		N		U		BREAK	

LZT	Mike:	I have received the following message from agents.
TCD	Romeo:	Party?
VHX	Mike:	Saturday night
OAR	Romeo:	Happy to hear it or that
FS	Mike:	Be very careful in your intercourse with strangers
YCG	Romeo:	I do not trust too much to my _____
EZF	Mike:	Article indicated can be supplied, but it will require fitting. I will lend what is required
QNA	Romeo:	All precautions have been taken
TCD	Mike:	Proceed to rendezvous
FY	Romeo:	Hot bearings
TIV	Mike:	By no means plain
SDQ	Romeo:	What is her name?
SDL	Juliet:	My name is
J		Juliet
ENC		dazzling, am, is, are
SDT		What is your name?
SLD	Romeo:	My name is
R		Romeo
EBQ	Juliet:	Your name is not on my list; spell it alphabetically
JG	Romeo:	I wish to have personal communication with you
IJ	Juliet:	Unless your communication is very important, I must be excused
JM	Mike:	Stranger is suspicious
MYX	Romeo:	Fine day
EBL	Juliet:	I beg to be excused
PCF	Romeo:	The ice is so solid I cannot break through; send help
YCS	Mike:	Try again
H	Romeo:	Stop, heave to, or come nearer, I have something to communicate
USX	Juliet:	Sorry, I am unable to comply with your request
AGS	Romeo:	The following is plain language
TQB	Juliet:	I doubt if it is possible
RIC	Romeo:	Cannot make it out
EQO	Mike:	I decline to have anything further to say or do in the matter.
KUM		Nothing to be depended upon beyond your own resources
DJX		Farewell. Adieu (Mike leaves)

NM	Romeo:	I am on fire
MLI		You must not or cannot make any excuse
TMV		Shall I have the pleasure to or of
F		Foxtrot
FBX	Juliet:	As you please
QRA		I am willing to
T		Tango
QAW	Romeo:	It is very kind of you
FIG		At last
B		Bravo
OYP	Juliet:	Horny
BKS		Idiot
IVL		You are too close. Keep farther off.
DN		I have orders for you not to touch
HFL	Romeo:	Will you breakfast with me?
LS	Juliet:	It is not safe to go so fast
LAX	Romeo:	Will you dine with me?
MIL		Tomorrow evening
TQB	Juliet:	I doubt if it is possible
MIK	Romeo:	This evening?
LAW	Juliet:	What time is dinner or when will dinner be ready?
FBM	Romeo:	As soon as it is dark
DCA	Juliet:	With pleasure. I will accept.
MHL		A small establishment
HAJ	Romeo:	Cafe. Restaurant
DOQ	Juliet:	What would you recommend?
TUN	Romeo:	Preserved soup
GDC		Fresh beef and vegetables
STJ		Potato
IOG		Cheese
ISD		Ale, beer
BSU	Juliet:	We shall have
WVR		Sherry
SYR		Are any oysters to be had?
LMT		Half dozen
QXT		Lobster
ZGE		Rhine wine

OEZ		Goose
UWS		Rice
SCN		Mushroom
ZGB		Burgundy wine
TUJ		Preserved fruit
KC		Champagne
WIZ	Romeo:	Bicarbonate of soda
DZI		Have been short on allowance for some time
GKI		Can I get a bill cashed here?
IVK		Will you keep close to me during the night?
OXY		Hope you will
OXW	Juliet:	Hope you can
IP	Romeo:	Shall we keep company?
ITY	Juliet:	A visit from a Protestant clergyman would be much valued
GHI	Romeo:	Will you lead into or point out a good berth?
IHL	Juliet:	When do lay days commence?
DQU	Romeo:	After dinner
ZMD	Juliet:	Your zeal has been particularly noted by _____
MIR	Romeo:	Have you ever?
MIG	Juliet:	Every evening
KIQ		Every day. Daily
MJA		Every opportunity
NWC		Have you a proper certificate of competency?
TU	Romeo:	Have you a clean bill of health?
GHI		You are in a very fair berth
GIA	Juliet:	This is my best point
SHJ		Some swell
XOR	Romeo:	Thank you
GDS		May I begin to?
GIT	Juliet:	The sooner the better
MFO	Romeo:	Entrance is difficult
MFD	Juliet:	Try to enter
KZU	Romeo:	I am in difficulties; direct me how to steer
OOX	Juliet:	You should swing and enter stern first
HBK	Romeo:	What is the nature of the bottom or what kind of bottom have you?
HAY	Juliet:	Double bottom
FHR	Romeo:	Stern way. Going astern

LK	Juliet:	Go astern easy. Easy astern
ODI	Romeo:	I am going full speed
HC	Juliet:	It is not safe to go so fast
KZY	Romeo:	It is difficult to extricate
BK	Juliet:	Is anything the matter
VLA	Romeo:	Cock broken or damaged
EHR	Juliet:	What do the cost of repairs amount to?
DF	Romeo:	With some assistance I shall be able to set things to rights
AN	Juliet:	Are you in a condition to proceed?
CCQ	Romeo:	If it comes on to blow
NZ	Juliet:	Blowing hard
CCO	Romeo:	Blowing too hard
DIR	Juliet:	Can you renew the action?
PEO		According to the usual practice?
BKS	Romeo:	I shall, or will if I can
VKE	Juliet:	Can you lift your screw?
MIV	Romeo:	Every exertion has been made
SPG		Operations have commenced
CWY	Juliet:	You
ERH		Screw well
JCG	Romeo:	Are you coming?
JDG	Juliet:	I shall come off by and by or at the time indicated
OWT	Romeo:	I fear I cannot hold out much longer
X	Juliet:	Stop carrying out your intentions and wait for my signals
MZJ	Romeo:	When will you or it be finished?
JDH	Juliet:	I will come
JCQ	Romeo:	Come directly, immediately
JDC	Juliet:	Coming at once
LCO	Romeo:	Discharging
ZHC		Shall or will be withdrawn
DIR	Juliet:	Can you renew the action?
AI	Romeo:	I will not abandon you. I will remain by you
WGD	Juliet:	Sleep, sleepy, sleeping, slept
DXY	Romeo: Juliet:	All snug

EDQ   Any chance of war?
ODV   Good chance
IKF   No chance of peace
YU   Has war commenced?
YX   War has commenced
YW   War between ____ and ____ has commenced
KDX   How is the crop?
KDW   Crops have suffered severely
KDV   Crops destroyed
TN   Are you in want of provisions?
LHE   Distressed for want of food
YU   Want food immediately
NV   Unable for want of
YZ   Are you in want of water?
LHF   Distressed for want of water
NRC   Fresh water
YVH   No water to be had
NF   Dying from want of water
FJX   Have you been attacked?
NJ   I am attacked. I want assistance. Help, I am attacked
FO   Are you in danger?
NL   I am in danger
KLF   Much danger
KLE   In great danger
DNE   Enemy is advancing
DNA   Army is advancing
EQB   Is anyone wounded?
RKN   Many wounded
ZIN   How many wounded?
PKN   No. of killed and wounded not yet known
ZIM   How are the wounded?
YGJ   Without arms
FGX   Without assitance
YL   Want immediate medical assistance
CP   Cannot assist

NC	In distress. Want immediate assistance
CX	No assistance can be rendered. Do the best you can for yourselves.
GBT	I shall bear up
GBV	May I, or can I bear up?
YE	Want assistance
GLN	Want bread
RZX	Want more support
LHI	How long have you been in such distress?
KNG	How many days?
RKD	Many
RKQ	So many
RKS	Too many
KLD	How many have you dangerously ill?
LQN	Dying at the rate of _____ a day
ZIE	Could, or might be worse
ZIF	It will be worse
ZIG	Much worse
MSK	Is my family well?
ZBM	Not so well
FZB	When was the battle fought?
KBN	Daylight. At daylight
KOY	When was the last death?
FIB	Daybreak. Dawn. At dawn
KOM	How many dead?
KON	Who is dead?
KOU	Dearer, dearest
KOV	Too dear

RJE   man
DWS   alderman
GVL   boatman
IFD   cattleman
TUO   chairman
ITX   clergyman, parson or minister
MDK   have you men enough?
NAB   fireman
NBS   fisherman
NJX   foreman
OTR   helmsman
RKI   how many men?
QIB   landsman
QJL   leadsman
QPJ   liberty man
RAE   look-out man look out!
NSX   he, or she is full of men
RPH   newly raised man
SIT STILLnobleman
TQO   postman
UXF   rifleman
VLG   seaman
WDH   signalman
YZM   tradesman
YWH   waterman
ZIA   workman
MDK   have you men enough?
RPJ   want men
RPK   your men

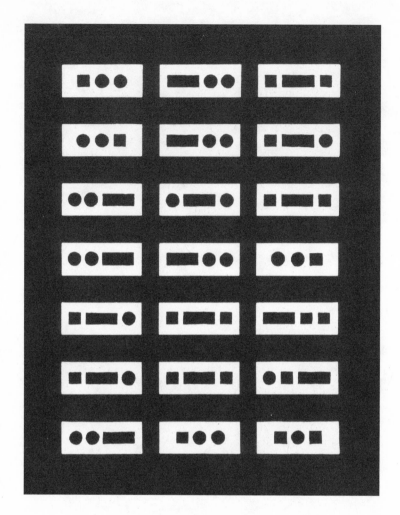

QRD   Light

LRG   Will you carry a light?
MPD   Will you make the land tonight?
LRM   I will carry a light
GDW   I see the land, land in sight
GDV   I have just lost sight of the land or light
MQC   Anything in sight?

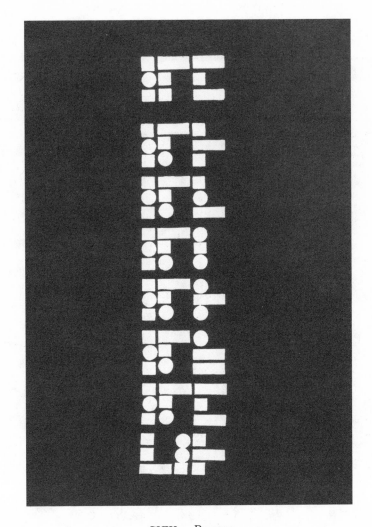

CHW   PIRATES

CJD   I was plundered by a pirate

CJF   Describe the pirate

CJN   She is armed

CJP   How is she armed?

CJS   She has long guns

CJW   I have no long guns

BLD   I am a complete wreck

TMQ	If you please
ZGS	Do you wish to?
FBX	As you please
ZGU	If you wish
ZGV	It is my wish
LBG	Will person please?
QTR	I or persons indicated wish to see you
ZGW	Wish to speak to you
TMW	Will you please?
ZGX	Wish you would
USR	Request the pleasure of
OCA	With pleasure. I will accept
TMU	Shall I have the pleasure to or of?
DBX	Very acceptable
OAP	Will you give me the pleasure?
TMX	With much pleasure
ZJQ	Will you write?
ZLH	Yes, I will
WRY	Will you stay or wait?
HUG	Yes, I can
JEA	Will you accompany?
DCZ	I will accompany
JGV	Will you give me the pleasure of your company at?
JGT	Very glad of your company
JGS	The pleasure of your company
TIR	I or persons indicated gratefully accept

ZGB	Another—some other
QGD	Any person or thing
QGF	Some
QGH	The
QGJ	Both
QGK	Each
QGL	Every. Every one. All
QGM	Nothing
QGN	More
QGP	Much. Many
QGR	Not so much. Less
QGS	From
QGT	On
QGV	On the _____
QGW	On me
QHB	On you
QHC	On (person-s indicated)
QHD	With
QHF	And
QHG	For
QHJ	For me
QHK	For you
QHL	For (persons indicated)
QHM	In. Into
QHN	To
QHP	To be
QHR	Why?
QHS	How?

BEA   Am. I Am

BEC   Am I?
BED   Am I not?
BEF   Am I to?
BYG   How am I?
CUY   Why am I?
CUA   Why are you?
CUZ   Why are (or is)?
CUX   Why?
CPV   What, or Which am I?
CSǪ   Where am I (or, are we)?

COT   Was I?
COU   Was I not?
BFR   Had, or Have I been?
BFH   Can, or May have been

BHC   Shall, or Will I be?
BHG   Shall, or Will we be?
BIX   Will it be?
BHE   Shall, or Will there be?

BFP   Could, or Might there be?
BFI   Can, or May there be?
BKH   Can, or May I be?
BFC   Am, Are, or Is to be?
BFE   Be the
BGY   Let us be

RAT   Can (Able to)

HJM   I can
HJN   I can be
CSB   He, She, It or _____, can be
CSR   They, or _____s, can be
CSJ   Can he, she, it or _____? be?
CSK   Can I?
CLS   Can I be?
CSM   Can I do anything for you?

BVZ   It

FAO   As it is
FAR   As it was
FAS   As it was not
FAU   As it will be
CDF   Is it?
PTN   It is as
BGR   It ought to be
BGT   It shall (or will) be
BGU   It shall (or will) not be
BNV   It will do
BIX   Will it be?
BOU   Will it do?
CQG   What or which is it?
CDY   Its-self (see also he, she, it or person-s or thing-s indicated)

LWC	Follow me
LWF	Will you lead?
LWG	Will you follow?
LWJ	Shall I follow?
LWK	I will follow
LWC	Follow me
LWF	Will you lead?
LWG	Will you follow?
LWJ	Shall I follow?
LWK	I will follow
LWC	Follow me
LWF	Will you lead?
LWG	Will you follow?
LWJ	Shall I follow?
LWK	I will follow
LWC	Follow me
LWF	Will you lead?
LWG	Will you follow?
LWJ	Shall I follow?
LWK	I will follow
LWC	Follow me
LWF	Will you lead?
LWG	Will you follow?
LWJ	Shall I follow?
LWK	I will follow
LWC	Follow me
LWF	Will you lead?
LWG	Will you follow?
LWJ	Shall I follow?
LWK	I will follow
LWC	Follow me
LWF	Will you lead?
LWG	Will you follow?
LWJ	Shall I follow?
LWK	I will follow
LWC	Follow me
LWF	Will you lead?

TQA   POSSIBLE-ITY

TQB	I doubt if it is possible
FRW	Barely possible
TQD	Is it possible?
TQE	Possibly
TQF	Quite possible
FBJ	As slow as possible
FBG	As quick as possible
FAI	As fast as possible
FBO	As soon as possible
FAY	As much (or, many) as possible
TQC	If possible
FOU	Avoid, if possible (impossible)
PFB	Not possible

CME   THE

BEN	Are, or Is the _____?
BFE	Be the _____
BJU	By the _____
HUE	Can, or may the _____?
BLF	Could, or Might the _____?
BMK	Do, Does or Did the _____?
BPG	For the _____
BPS	From the _____
BQX	Had, Has or Have the _____?
BZY	If the _____
CDN	In the _____
CEY	Must the _____?
CGA	Not the _____
CGR	Of the _____
CHD	On the _____
CHV	Ought the _____?
CJT	Should, or would the _____?

CSQ   WHERE AM I (OR, ARE WE)?

CSQ	Where am I (or, are we)?
WJV	Somewhere
CST	Where are they?
DQR	Anywhere
CSR	Where are (or, is)?
MJC	Everywhere
SI	Where are you from?
EQS	Anywhere else
SH	Where are you bound?
LVS	Elsewhere
CSR	Where is?
CSP	Whereabouts

TRANS-SPACE COMMUNICATION

I am interested in exploring methods of communication that will be understood face to face, or at any distance, regardless of language, country or planet or origin, by all sending and receiving.

For three years I have used the International Code of Signals to make poems and poetry events, because this code makes available and possible the translation of simultaneous equivalents:

flashing light (by morse): abstract visual

sound signaling (by morse): abstract aural

live semaphore: motion

fixed semaphore: motion

flag hoists: concrete visual

radio: electronic

words (including equivalent translations in seven different languages)

I consider this code an exploration of linear communication, which has served the binary neurological function of the brain. The most useful thing for me here, in the code, is the understanding of the equivalents: one kind of signal may equally be substituted for another with the exact same meaning. It then becomes very clear when a different, non-linear thinking appears, as in "knight's thinking" (schizophrenic thinking). Here, as in the chess game, the move is two up in a linear fashion, but then one jump to the side, to a conclusion or a connection that may baffle the listener if he is expecting a linear-causal relationship.

Lately my own explorations have dealt with the use of minimal clues: how much information can be received, and how accurately, through how little means. For example, a television set with its back to the audience and no sound on represents an equivalent translation of movement into light through an electronic medium but offers little information; (negative shadows?). Half a Ping Pong game may readily give the nature of the whole, half a telephone conversation may not. When is movement a more efficient means of communication than words? For what complexities of thought? Do different complexities require different methods of communication? And how do we judge when to use what?

The amount of information available has more than doubled since World War II. In the next ten years it will double again. How do we deal with it?

1. Do we use more than the 5% of the brain now in use?

2. Do we process quicker?

3. Do we decode information more and put it in another form (not language) so that the present brain can handle it?

4. Is there a change in the neural circuits of the brain?

If the last, is this a change from a binary to an analog system in the brain? Is this a mutant? Is this a quantum jump to a different energy level? Is there a new form of communication to accomodate these changes? Is it here? Has it yet to be developed? Has it any relationship to "knight's thinking"? Has it any relationship to changes in so-called "states of consciousness"? Is it an analogous, circular, field or some other non-linear system?

What relation will this new form have, or has already, to the high incidence of television, telephone and other electronic communication, to users of LSD, to the fact that Dr. Sackett, at the University of Wisconsin, has discovered that monkeys reared in isolation have more adaptive learning facilities when the brain has been directly stimulated by electrodes?

At the moment I am interested in exploring methods of communication through space; considering space as space fields or space solids; through great distances of space; through small distances, such as the space between the nucleus and the electrons of an atom; through distances not ordinarily related to the form of communication used. I am interested in doing this so that we may develop methods of communication that will be understood face to face, or at any distance, regardless of language, country or planet of origin, by all sending and receiving. For me this implies an understanding of four, five, (and six?) dimensional space; of how what can be transmitted through this space; of how these spatial dimensions relate to different "states of consciousness" and to different neurological patterns (if any).

Send replies to:
Box 619
Woodstock, NY

The Fashion Show Poetry Event
by Eduardo Costa, John Perreault, and
   Hannah Weiner
January 14, 1969, 5:30 and 7:30
Center for Inter-American Relations
680 Park Avenue, New York, N.Y.

Poetry (Fashion Commentaries) by:
   Eduardo Costa, John Perreault, and
   Hannah Weiner

Fashion works by:
   James Lee Byars, Enrique Castro-Cid,
   Eduardo Costa, Allan D'Arcangelo,
   Rubens Gerchman, Alex Katz, Les
   Levine, Nicholas Krushenick, Roberto
   Plate, Marisol, Sylvia Stone, Andy
   Warhol, Susana Salgado, John
   Perreault, Marjorie Strider, Claes
   Oldenburg, James Rosenquist, Hannah
   Weiner, Alfredo Rodriguez Arias, and
   Juan Stoppani.

Music by: Davin Seay and Diane Kolisch

THE FASHION SHOW POETRY EVENT ESSAY

"There is no more aesthetic contemplation because aesthetics is
dissolving itself into social life."   —Octavio Paz

"Clothing introduced perfidy into civilization. But without clothing
could they (the primitive peoples) have taught themselves to think?"
         —Claude Levi-Strauss

    We see the Fashion Show Poetry Event not as a time-bounded work of literature,
but as the initial cause of a series of events which are a set of translations that add up to a
total work.

    Some of these additional events are The Fashion Show Poetry Event #2—a re-
creation using video tapes, slide projections, and stereo tapes—and the Fashion Show
Poetry Event Book which will be a "documentation" in words and photographs including
the texts of our fashion description poems, our press releases, magazine articles, etc.

It might have been interesting for us to have asked the artists to tell us orally an idea for a fashion garment and then for us to have written our texts without making and showing the real garments.

However, some of the reasons we chose to make the effort of presenting an actual fashion show were: to move outside the limitations of the printed word, to move away from personal expression, and to present a fictionalized version of a real life event that would appeal to an audience accustomed to sophisticated perception of visual phenomena.

Rather than attempt a union of our three separate styles we have chosen an objective mass-media style. This makes a difference of kind rather than of degree between our present effort and other forms of literary collaboration.

Concerning the total phenomenon of fashion as a language, we would locate the Fashion Show Poetry Event in the area of that particular sub-category of fashion language that could be characteristic of the moment of communication between fashion press and fashion show to consumer.

Fashion language is a complicated code. It has special meanings within the industry itself, involving the translation of exact equivalents, and special meanings when the industry relates to the public.

There are various verbal (written and oral) to visual and visual to verbal translations that take place in the Fashion Show Poetry Event.

We wish to indicate some differences between translation and communication. In the process of communication there is a sender, a message, and a receiver. Between sender and receiver some modification of the message may take place even though, for instance, the message is in the English language which is known equally to both sender and receiver.

On the other hand, translation is a process of converting a message from one code system to another (from one medium to another or one language to another).

We communicated to the artists our generalized instructions. They translated these instructions into sketches, models, and finally actual garments. The feedback (i.e. the garments) was then translated by us into fashion language. We have also translated this information into the language of press releases aimed at both the general and the fashion press and into the language of this theoretical essay.

This process of translation is one of the most important subjects of The Fashion Show Poetry Event.

The message received by the usual fashion audience and by most of the poetry and art audience as well will be mainly a certain set of meanings. The real message and the message we intend, however, is the game or play of the significants that will transmit an additional set of meanings.

There is a difference between a description and that which this description appears to describe. We are interested in this difference.

There is a difference between real fashion copy and our "poems" which are imitations of fashion copy. There is a difference between a real fashion show and our imitation of a fashion show. We are interested in these differences in spite of the fact that we have tried to eliminate them.

We want to show the difference between presentation and representation by bringing presentation and representation as close together as possible.

The Fashion Show Poetry Event is not only fashion, poetry, and art, it is where these arbitrary categories overlap and as categories dissolve and become irrelevant.

The Fashion Show Poetry Event is a new kind of theater.

Theater is a fictional representation of something that supposedly happened in the past or something that is happening in the present. A real fashion show is a fictional representation of something that is going to happen in the future. The FSPE is a fiction of this kind of fictional representation.

In theater, costumes are usually subservient to plot and characterization. In the theater of the FSPE, as in a real fashion show, the costumes *are* the plot.

We caused fashion garments to be created by the artists so that we would have a pretext to write the style of fashion.

We use the phrase "write the style" rather than the more usual "write *in* the style" because the latter indicates that one is using a style to serve a certain content, but here we are writing a certain style using a certain content as a pretext to write this style.

Not only are we writing the style of written fashion language, we are also doing the style of a fashion show. This makes our work a poetry event instead of a poetry reading.

Because the Fashion Show Poetry Event is amusing does not exclude the fact that it is also serious. Amusement and beauty in this work are nothing but the condition of the style we are writing and doing, as is fashionableness.

The fact that the audience and we ourselves will find this work amusing is also amusing.

Doing a fashion show is fashionable. The artists we have chosen are fashionable. Poetry events are fashionable. Fashion is fashionable. Fashionableness is not our goal. Our goal is complete objectivity.

obligated hannah weiner reading two class make clear you were an opposite i met ted in
the spring of 1964 wearing blue at the metro cafe down on ol second avenue   he was with
sandy a baby wearing one red he never changed the color sweater   he was the first poet i
met on the streets   i had just at 35 started to write and was taking kenneth koch's class at
the new school and had been well read in koch ohara and ashbery as contemporaries but
ted was the first real contemporary poet for me   he was welcome in my house at all times
that summer i read the sonnets and i realized the revolution was in the streets   next year
we were in berkeley together, he was reading at the poetry conference, with ed sanders
and also and i took it as a vacation from my underwear design job   he says he slept in my
hotel room he kept warm but i only remember him he said biting my toes good girl stupid
he was taking a bath   he spent the night after frank oharas funeral at my east hampton
we record personal details   house   drinkin the other stuff   hannah they wonder we talked
all night being irish and woman   hannah that means you met him a long time ago   yes
almost 20 years and a lifetime of the poetry he was second   we were different   he worked
somewhat dillettantely and i suffragette   he was a clear understanding of the worker street
problem   he never cried   at my house we discussed the formal problems   he was lying
down   hannah he would laugh   big bear   he was gone and the day i cried for it bellyful
signed at the above i was a contemporary and i was pushed keep it clear on the streets we
are workin two poets are already insit off

who is impossible as a leader   who is jackson   speaker
on the whole front page   continuance   often teach   silent
too   horse carriage for sir elder
please sir older we grow we know more older

jackson the perfect scream   lists puzzles good dictionaries
too much quote   do out   jackson please breakdow   dont
erase jackson thats funny quote

has have   good for you take jackson out   EAT   dear jackson
said dont drink

experiment in any form that occurs to jackson

you hear jacksons voice   CHAREMAGNE   jackson is obvious
ridiculous wrong   calling window level OOLONG   big bok

just say jacksons voice reread heard   ohboy permit   life
granted twice   what yer sayin   what yer sayin   read also
he hears me when i read   hear him too   also silent

ohboy dont get rid of that old man please   them boys and
girls   ohboy they learning fast   oh jackson

the plant that flashed is still flashing   so what   jackson
can see its energy field   its pretty   purply iridescent
oh jackso potato fields

remember the umbrella   it wanted you to take an umbrella
rain   you refused   it said get an umbrella   get the navy

blue one   jackson always carries one   he shows up with
umbrella at a reading   you both come out   WOW   it rains for
one minute   you both laugh

listen to jackson voice   obtrusion   complete line
be clever   hear jackson

                              clairvoyantly written
                              Hannah Weiner

Driving to NY with Anne and Michael and Ted while Bernadette goes East in a blue car and
Ed is still sleeping in bed.
Do not be relevant said Ted.
We bought 3 hamburgers
         1 BLT
         3 coffees
         2 cakes
         3 carvel sundaes
         4 sparkplugs
         4 gallons of gas
         1 toll
  made   3 ecological violations (3 carvel containers dumped on road)
   had   1 turquoise scarf (Ted)
         1 red hat (Anne)
         1 grey sweater (Michael)
         1 pr. blue boots (me)
Another World will appear soon edited by Anne. Anne gets out at St. Marks. Ted gets out
with Anne thinking of dinner with George and money for his mother from Steve. I get out
at Bernadettes. Michael drives off in the car.
The front door is open.
The loft door is open.
2 cats are there
I turn on 2 gas flames and make 2 phone calls.
I talk to Tina who comes home from work.
We eat cereal and fruit cake.
Tina wears my coat
I wear Tina's pants
I go to sleep in B & E's bed
Do not make lists, said Ted.

It is clear MY STATEMENT that these forces, words are a "guide to better living." The WORDS have political, ecological awareness, concern for others as well as myself, always suggesting a course that is to the most benefit of all concerned, to increase physical, psychological and mental well being, and reduce suffering. These forces also lead me to places of spiritual development, such as Satchidananda's retreats, the Providence Zen Center, etc. These forces describe themselves as WISDO, not enough TRIALS, room on my forehead for M! They joke. Some words are warnings rather than suggestions, i.e., they appear as negatives or oppositions. NOT CORRECT. Well, they used to. The words tell me when to turn on <u>WBAI</u>; when there is a war on; and I get messages visual and aural (the spacing is theirs) from both radio and TV. SMOKE. I light a cigarette even though I consider it bad for my lungs. Sometimes a word relating to the news will appear in the air MORE DETAILS follow on a news program: things to watch out for.

All these words occur whether I write or not, in my ordinary conscious state, not in a trance, and sometimes in sleep GET UPS appears on my forehead to wake me in time. FOR WHAT. Anything.

I am trying to understand through my continued writing which of these WORDS I see are 1) my own ordinary conscious thought; 2) from my developed superconscious mind which has precognitive, clairvoyant powers; 3) telepathic connections with living people; 4) BIG QUESTION communications from non-living forces.

The manuscript begins in the fall of 1970, describing a 3 week fast. The early material contains much information on the nature of the kundalini energy and electro magnetic sensitivity that I have never seen elsewhere. KNOWLEDGE. I was receiving FORCE messages through FEELING energy at that time. Later pictures developed, and colors. Then in Aug. 1972 words developed.

Unfortunately the fasting experience left my body weakened and I am still ill often and tire easily. I feel that I should spend my time working with this gift. MONEY. It leaves me without a source of income.

Living with these words is like living under orders. It always knows more than I do so I usually obey the directions, trying to put aside my personality, EGO, desires, habits, etc., except for fatigue which often stops me. The hardest thing to deal with was opposition in the use of language. They used best, prefer, necessary, good, important, to mean the opposite—this is explained in the few pages of Oct. 73 that I include in the ms. It was easy to give up material possessions, my loft, my habits of living, my position in the poetry-art world (I was too weak to do anything but stay home AND WRITE), but to change the habits of language created great anguish.

WELL REVIEWED

The words train me: DONT CHOOSE, DONT PRETEND, DONT COMPLAIN, DONT LIE, overcome emotions. In reading both the Seth Material and the Book of Urantia I notice my life with words seems to follow a course of learning described by them as occuring after death. I am incorporating part of that consciousness now. I very rarely have out of body (astral) experiences and I am not cognizant of past lives. I see no images of saints, yogis, etc., when I once cried because I wanted to see "the light" I saw the word BULB instead.

TRAINING

The development of language over the last BOOK makes things much clearer. The vocabulary has increased, as well as forms of language, different tenses, participles, etc. Also jokes on language as: GO TO SLEEPING. EAT A BAKED POTATOE. It has never modified potatoe with LIVING before. PLENTIFUL.

I am unusual, as far as I can discover, in having this extensive gift of SEEING language. I have met people who see words BACON occasionally. It has nitrate. It is more common to hear THANK YOU voices. What I see as words, others may experience as feeling cigarette or thought.

The four years of this manuscript document my experiences and changes in perception. I continue writing as a collaborator with WORDS I SEE. Sometimes I struggle, as I do not ENJOY all their interruptions. They edit the manuscript as well, and I have lately begun to edit them, for literary values.

OMIT

Their comment on this is O^k

3/10

How can I describe anything when all these interruptions keep *arriving* and then
tell me I dont describe it well   WELL *forgive them* big ME   COUNTDOWN
got that for days and yesterday it didn't stop GO TO COUNTDOWN GO TO
COUNTDOWN CALL DAVIDs get COUNTDOWN finally GO TO COUNT-
DOWN at the door so OK I go see these maroon velvet pants I'm not BUY $40
he isn't home
pants BLOOMINGDALES all over again I leave GO TO COUNTDOWN: refuge,
get in a taxi, start for home, no peace, get out GO TO COUNTDOWN ok it's only
money go back and buy the pants it's better than seeing GO TO COUNTDOWN
for the rest of my life *peace* so they fit well   UNTIL   MICHAEL COOPER
For a while I tried to get away with *negative* COUNTING   by counting down
10, 9, 8, 7   while breathing GO TO MAKE CLEARer   FAR OUT
B   at the door RHYS RHYS IMPORTANT (notes) HAVE A DOUBLE
L
I   image of pink embroidered pillow case appears on blanket, get it out
S
S   GO NOW *girlfiriend negative* MOTHER made it when I was 2
F   TATA
U   JANA   she's fasting TRY HARDER across her chest and
L   *eat enough*
              DRESS WARM across Charlemagne's groin   Joan's
                  head says LAUGHS as she   QUINK THICK   SAY IT
                            laughs
    Rhys *rhythm*   VERY IMPORTANT says radio   LY
        DESCRIBE *go ahead* in Charlemagne's white pants WOOL white hat
        IMITATED Hawai JOAN   ARAKAWA   (more notes going back 3 days)
                            well tho
YOU WONT OBEY   PORK CHOP BUY THEM *pig* in pork chop color along
the edge of   NOT APPLE PIE in pink and white sash
    frying
            ORGASM*deaf*ement go to a museum
        get exci JUNKtement*grapefruit*   CANT GET THE SPACING
                eat grapefruit   it's a nice arc
                    I T W R I T E S
                            I
                            T
                            S
Try praying: Our father who art *be right over*   E
A song: Here we go round the mulberry bush the   L F
grapefruit John the mulbery *mush* GIVE UP
GRAPEFRUIT" IS THE NAME OF Yoko Ono's book, APOLOGIZE is on a Ringo
Star2 record 2 r's   Call Jerry MISS ROTHENBERG MISS DAVID ANTIN
SNOWING IN VERMONT *delightful*   Dream about Jason Epstein very huge
                            JOHN
loud SHUT UP in hs office, *I rejoice*   laugh   DESCRIBE CHARLEMAGNE
how old 33 spiritual discipline
        not in dollars not too negative
            no money   MONEY

3/10 p 4

LAMONTE had this dream listening to Lamonte   GET ALREADY SCARED
STUPID NEXT before I can type it the *heals* carnations fall over water spills on floor,
wiping it see in the other part of *the room* a blue puddle just like the one spilled
says WATER   I laugh *far out*   YOUR notes
VERY SERIOUS LAMONTge*t*f*r*i

very serious operation   get *fri* *already scared*   LIVER   WHAT D'YA
THINK huge HER VOICE*dorothy*gh*te*   her voice is pretty clear sounds just
like her*liver*   CALL RAYMOND   *ned* his liver side flashed
Had trouble with my own just in time make some parsley tea? WHAT BOIL IT
IN WATER *stop* stop drinking wine? *Heal yourself* says stomach LAMONTE
didn't *e* maybe it is my thought had to look up to see if e Met Dorothy   where I
got my ulcer, *working hard* her voice *I'll hit you - direct hit*
Good heat vibrations in 1st chakra area WHEW *good idea*
maybe it will heal now   GOOD L$_U$CK just remembered
                                        Dorothy's healing group CONCENTRATE
on her   they have success healing

            told her about Le Shan, who trains healers GO TO ONE
                    Steve Reich is not tunafish   GOOD LUCK better fix the lock*no*
better   More notes: shopping go into supermarket much **interference, leave,** *ta ta*
cross 2nd ave *think of that* GOOD   resistance GO HOME I'm mad and hungry
no food in the house but LUCK   go home GOOD GIRL and then a huge STOP
in front of the butcher shop, meat cheaper and better   *big improvement* NO
on the expensive farmer's cheese, GO OUT, GET A HARD ROLL, CREAM
SUGAR   I get it they'd rather I didn't have either*milk tues*   Hear TURN IT
OFF (the oven) SOR*RY* says roll   Be quiet I say I'm eating breakfast   THATS
THE INTERFERENCE HAPPY YEAR TAKA *wrong recommend, feel different,*
missed his movies hear *feel awful*   OMIT APOSTROPHE   SACRIFICE   *try*
hard   Takas advice   omit apostrophe, Elianes   writes in the present tense see
PRESENT   say SEE not saw, *eliminates periods ol stupid girl*   Charlemagne's
address   big pink PREFER *this is terrific old girl*
                          thats the conclusion

I SEE A BIG APOSTROPHE

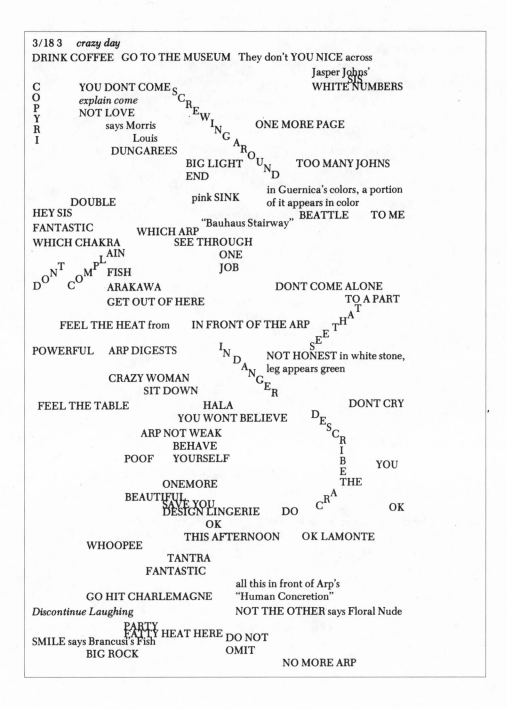

3/18 3   *crazy day*
DRINK COFFEE   GO TO THE MUSEUM   They don't YOU NICE across

Jasper Johns'
WHITE NUMBERS   SIS

C
O   YOU DONT COME   SCREWING
P   *explain come*   AROUND
Y   NOT LOVE
R   says Morris   ONE MORE PAGE
I   Louis
            DUNGAREES
                    BIG LIGHT   TOO MANY JOHNS
                    END
                                      in Guernica's colors, a portion
            DOUBLE   pink SINK   of it appears in color
HEY SIS
FANTASTIC   BEATTLE   TO ME
WHICH CHAKRA   WHICH ARP   "Bauhaus Stairway"
                  SEE THROUGH
          DONT COMPLAIN   ONE
                FISH   JOB
            ARAKAWA   DONT COME ALONE
            GET OUT OF HERE   TO A PART
                                                      THAT
      FEEL THE HEAT from   IN FRONT OF THE ARP
                                            SEE
POWERFUL   ARP DIGESTS   INDANGER   NOT HONEST in white stone,
                                      leg appears green
          CRAZY WOMAN
              SIT DOWN
  FEEL THE TABLE   HALA   DONT CRY
                YOU WONT BELIEVE   DESCRIBE
          ARP NOT WEAK
              BEHAVE
        POOF   YOURSELF
                                            YOU
                                          THE
              ONEMORE
        BEAUTIFUL   CRA
        SAVE YOU
          DESIGN LINGERIE   DO   OK
              OK
          THIS AFTERNOON   OK LAMONTE
      WHOOPEE
            TANTRA
          FANTASTIC
                          all this in front of Arp's
        GO HIT CHARLEMAGNE   "Human Concretion"
Discontinue Laughing   NOT THE OTHER says Floral Nude
        PARTY
        FATTY HEAT HERE DO NOT
SMILE says Brancusi's Fish
      BIG ROCK   OMIT
                        NO MORE ARP

67

April 17 *Nick's advice*   *informal*   *reach the important level*   MORE POWER H I L EV E L *more*
tooth
calories Diderot Nick is exhausted   *get drunk*   *see yourself* you M A D H concen-
THIS IS MEDITATION
trate *on Nick* he relaxes   you get high *seventh important one* S A M   more year
Fall River VISIT RIMPOCHE   *more tooth*
not kidding   FOUR DOLLARS you give   YOU'RE OK C H *try for Bernadette cry*
it's the combination   *feel OK* energy released in back R E A NOT RELAXED *see*
                                          ½ *of it*
David *wear the pants* *get out of it*   across chest   *for me dont cancel*
no longer NOT OK   *in vaudeville* see *the tooth* next   says upper left tooth
                        in Connecticut   *crotch*   *learn the tricks of the trade* *get an diction*
                                                                                    penmanship
                                                                                   auditor ary
WEAR DUNGAREES USE THE FIRST PERSON I, THE PERSON, put on the
baggy dungarees *feel the energy jacket*   *too intense* stomach hurts more pain
Not because theyre baggy NO MORE   you eat *yea cramps* THROW THEM
OUT dungarees take them off feel better   STOMACH
                B E R N A D E T T E

        COOL HIM OUT   *table talks* cover it, stop eating or THROW OUT
SAMADHI *big cool*   BEAUTIFUL   huge letters come in *pussy cat*
       you'll survive
Malcolm is in England *Sorry about Rhys* meditating SIT FOR RHYS made no
                                                                      wish
LUCKY connection   The old kitchen table *on the kitchen floor*   SO OBVIOUS
throw it out COME BACK HERE Meditating   *refrigerator*   with Dorothy's
sense   penis emergency DONT OBEY healing group see NORA, AMHERST
BACK across the shoulder, GALL BLADDER SAFE NOW   *Xray* The old table
                                                          see eyelashes
is good for the typewriter? It wobbles It *types* *last night* STOP ME says the
top of the casing the whole thing vibrates *you didn't finish* GOODBYE says the
window IT GETS STOLEN, says the window COLDCREAM ON THE
LEDGE there's PUT FLOWERS OUT on a wide curved ledge PIECE *more*
confident correct height of table? *sure* WEAR EYE MAKEUP IT'S SPRING
MAKE IT CORRECT TOO MANY STOPS THE ENERGY INCREASES   CALL
CHARLEMAGNE at midnight? NOT ON THE PHONE COFFEE NOT THE
CORRECT POSITION   DEADLOCK does that mean FOX IT DOES FIX THE
TABLE   *Not another* APOLOGIZE PLEASE APOLOGIZE NOA   YOUR
BROTHER'S CALLING SALARY IMPORTANT NOVEL the underlining
                                           be a victim
stopped with the typewriter on the low table PUT IT BACK   BIG IMPROVE-
MENT the keys are under our chin *reach Samadhi level* call Josh? *Reynolds*
You didn't Rhys tonight meditate on him after finishing *make an appt* with
Dorothy's *lunch*   good grief you go CRAZY PRESIDENT Dorothy's voice   *see*
a picture of the typewrite on
         the little table

April 17 p 2   *apologize to Rhys*   BIG APPLE   MODERN ART THURS
                                      WEAR   IMPORTANT
John Ashbery reads, Ron Padgett   NOA'S VOICE: LOW INCOME GO TO
BOSTON, COUNTING ONCE NOT FRIENDS *big victim not terrible*
explain the locks: one fox lock that doesn't work, one slip lock easy *understand* STAY IN THE HOSPITAL
girlfriend
to break, one police floor   NOT USEFUL *bar* FIX THE BAR
Then there's a deadbolt the city could put in   IT ANSWERS   What's the
answer to Noa we don't see each other MUCH DONT GO HOME TO ENGLAND
Problem money   *be careful* *clothes* *good for you* *feel Malcolm*   RHYS AT
                              witches   *now luck*
SAMADHI LEVEL   Nothing jumps into the bath   *too much starch*
take it back   MUCH SAFER in cucumber juice thinking of CALCIUM
     juice

                              THURS
                           GO TO BED

appreciate it Michael calls early *asleep* call back SO MUCH SETBACK the black
GO TO SLEEP   1:30 IT'S A SIMPLE AFTERNOON **BRAVO** *This is Michael*
NOW TRUTH   GO HANNAH a huge one in front of the typewriter, where you
were setting in the sun not OK GO OUTSIDE   *Windowsill*   but it says NO as
       design lingerie
you get the jacket   Wondering whether to wear the scarf or not, Bernadette calls
anger NO NICK SCARF   that must be her opinion *BLESS YOU* she always
wears one SIT DOWN smoke a little*an hour goes by you're ok* *not simple go to*
                                                           the museum of mod
HELP *best issue you're kidding* j*a* wear scarf GOOD FOR   *not for you art*
YOU *Larry jokes* GOOD AFTER*k*et s*c* NOON   STOP THIS NONSENSE
                                  arf

STOP TH SENTENC

M 4 p 2

realize write something you are documenting it   no sex appeal   3 more ears
you hear GINSENG over the
radio, rather than see it   You buy a plant that flashed even after it said IT WAS
JUPITER
A WARNING you've been up since 7 and haven't stopped yet   You heard it
when you bought ice cream   WHY   CHEWING GUM   *movie*   WHY BUS STOP
GET GINSENG YOU HAVE TIME When *go to sleep* you come in the door it says
MENTAL ASTRAL   A 60 FT long CHARLEMAGNE across the parking lot
FRONT DOOR ONE MORE PHIL the cat ate a yellow tulip   The plant that
flashed is still flashing *so what* Jackson you can see it's energy field   It's pretty
Purply iridescent   you had some GET OUT   KLEENEX some psychic healers
milk
do kleenex operations the kleenex disappears into the body and is retrieved with
junk on it   YOUR WORDS   You take some white flowers out leave a few AT
THE JAPANESE   Phil calls NOT LOUD GET THE PAPERS PLEASE BELIEVE
is that why ESE   LEVEL you got the Sunday paper   the only time in WHEN
contact
and Nothing fell out the window because you were TOOTS   You get another
plant SUNMUR says forehead YOU HEAT YOU   LOOK AT THE LIVING
ROOM   PHOTOGRAPH *no foolin* hear CALCIFYING in hall cant get voice
not Jim's   BIG DREAM says mother's photo NOT YOURS   The duplicated
manuscript says *think of it* NO   *go hannah*   *money* and louder MONEY *his voice
hungry* Your mother's photograph says DID *BED* YOU HAVE A NICE TIME
DONT GO
LAST NIGHT   GIANTS   CALL JANA 533 NOT HOME says forehead
PLEASE YOURSELF TONIGHT *your emotions*   Noa   sees her thoughts *in
abstract* colors   SHE RESENTS IT like films the subconscious mind in little
pictures in the WALK back of her head and the bigger ones out front NEGA DO
THEY CORRECT YOUR POSTURE she said yes she had to CERTAIN look at
them from a certain angle   NOT BREATH GET OVER IT *not sure of it* around
head in her BOOMERANG *your empty* apt   She takes aspirin   YOU DID twice
last night HURT SELF   *Not tenderloin*   You get *contact* apple turnovers, beer
also NEGATIVE it said CONTACT before who got beer?   It goes *danger*
go out for two hours   NEGATIVE
BIG APPLE PIE is beginning to appear over words that are negative no you know
Merry Christpetticoat   SYS   You hear/see WEAR DUNGAREES many times
neg on street STREET WEAR HARDLY anyone you know wears them NOW
LAY DOWN WAIT LIPSTICK   as you look to the bedroom MUST NAP work on
confident
movie script   1 MORE HOUR   these 1 mores   Bought some flowering plants
for the window sill PRETTY FLOWERS says GRASS   Nothing bit your left
nipple twice last night OH GOOD Noa   says witches used to have an extra tit
under their left arm for the devil NO BEER Told her *witches go away* it was as

close as you *naked* could come

Big Peet

Wait a second

Thurs June 6   BIG PEET   *Noa thanks you*   *Big pick up*

You use COLD CREAM *you're in trouble* does the rain WASH AWAY? You go to
Medicaid the line is busy   BLOOMINGDALES, look for pants DONT SPOIL
THE DAY GET A LIGHT BULB you DONT the pants are all $& *Radcliffe hurts
get dungarees* GIVE UP look *crazy* at a raincoat GET A SECOND HAND ONE:
at a blouse, GO TO BOGIES antique clothes *take back Rhys* IS COMING NOT
FOR YOU walk south AT THE EMOTIONAL LEVEL   NOT CHEAP BIG
PEET you leave LEVER go for a cheap suitcase pass a store NOT SAFER on the
sidewalk go back COME IN HERE there's one GET THE SAME BRAND,
another brand is water-proof with lock, $5 *that a boy* GARISH well it's orange
and beige CHINATOWN RHYS IS COMING *you get exhausted* it's *bathing suit*
not true come home POTATOE CHIPS YOU MISS RHYS you always get
instructions to buy something orange before a retreat YOU MISS NOTHING says
home drink beer take a bath typing OH HANNAH an announcement for 7:30
you wait   go to the beach   COFFEE DRUNK says the kitchen   *dont ask
eat dinner alone*
you emanate you look tired   outside *the president's* apt you know you can go
touch Rhys in UP you quit YOU CAN TYPE   you DRUNK SAMADHI YOU
JANUARY SELFISH CORNER you nap GO OUT AT 10 G SOON   Home:
PHIL GLASS   ONE MIND   HIS MIND HIS CLARITY WE LOVE YOU
Phil Glass HIS MUSIC DONT CHOOSE MONEY HIS WORK VERY IMPOR-
TANT VERY SPECIAL BE SPECIAL POSTUM he drinks postum *cancer not me*
YOU FIND OUT RHYS *3 concerts* didn't KNOW about Dickie Landry's FOOL
didn't go to Sonnabend didn't see a poster TOO LATE SHOP Phil's voice TAKE
MONEY BIG TRIP   Phil *warning* gives you a record YOU DONT JOKE
MAKE EVERYBODY RHYS **W** you walked through RHYS *connecticut* & a big
W to Paula Cooper's no one there you hear SPRING go the Byrd's see John Marron
WALK WITH LAUGH JOHN YOU ARE A BIRD get a signal to leave see BErna-
dette? GO SOON get *LEWIS* a signal walk quit HANNAH NO MORE RHYS HE
DOESN'T APPEAR you PHIL AND SIMONE QUIT TYPING WHO TOLD YOU
TO SMOKE   THESE VOICES you go to the bedroom not pleasant CHEESE *an
empty room* YOU MUST FOLLOW *eat cheese* MEET   at the natural *foods
restaurant* NO NAME DONT LEAVE PHIL AND SIMONE *dont type* GLASS
YOU FOLLOW EVERYTHING TAKE MORE CALCIUM remember HIS
MONEY ONE MORE CHAKRA DONT PUBLISH IT You *feel tired* leaving
Phil's you hear his voice say CARCINOMA *cigarette* 3 MORE YEARS and *cancel*
when Bernadette calls see CANCER in air   WHO   *It's the month that might*
be cancer but not carcinoma you're depressed it's Friday WHO HAS cancer
NESIUM   *magne*   GO SOON TO THE BOWERY
                BARRY CANT PRINT

Sun June 9 p 2

It does hatha, YOU CAN LIVE LONG IT ISN'T PREDETERMINED JACK IS A
SERIOUS OMISSION   It didn't get *back* to Soltanoff   SEE DANGER ON
SUNDAY   NO OMISSION   NECK at concert it would like MONDAY to have
neck adjustment   CIRCLE exercise?   It rolls it's neck around slowly TAKE IT
EASY it is IT'S LAUGHING Bed it's 10 to 8   YOU COME HOME YOUR
OBEDIENCE TRIALS ARE OV.R.   no TRIALS YOU ARE AN OBEDIENT
7:30
miss E.
GIRL   This because you left Bernadette's when it said GO SOON GO SOON
GO GO GO and a shout OUT you left *go to fourth st   ta ta* you ONE O CLOCK
YOU TRY BEGIN Phoebes BAR it says *you go home* it goes to TIN PALACE
which reads GO TO PHOEBES LOVER and LEAVE   *takes a blanket* a
sleeping bag from DRINK Ed's loft *you saw Bernadette* and Ed and Ed *Friedman*
the movies girl TAKE THE SHORT CUT that's straight *across town* YOU SIT
WITH ED BOWES   NOTHING IS SURE OF ITSELF   YOU GET Ed's VOICE
BOWERY   PLEASE SIT DOWN YOUR PLANTS NEED WATER BERNA-
DETTE YOUR VOICE IS TRUE FABULOUS   YOUR OBEDIENCE
BECAUSE OF FRANCIS at the loft it hears BERNADETTE CALL it calls it GO
BREAKDOWN   B R E A K D O W N   *friend*   YOU CAN GO
HOME GO TO SLEEP GO TO A MOVIE YOUR OBEDIENCE CALLS
FRANCIS THIS WAKES HER UP   IT GETS TWO PAIR some confusion only
one fits   pair of Chinese pajama pants from Barry SHUT UP *very comfortable* one
is much too large BED first it said DONT TAKE THEM the black ones and then
dont go to
SHUT UP GO SOON IS COMING HERE TUESDAY everyone leaves town
YOUR OK YOU OBEY IT OBEYS YOU YOUR OK YOUR PETER THANKFUL,
THRAMBAL *you meet again* bar says *thank you* BUS   TOOTSIE GIRL YOUR
Frankenstein
MONEY   BED NO SOON YOU TAKE DICTATION YOU GO SOON   NO
MORE ACUPUNCTURE YOU FRIEND YOU TAKE THE WORLD A
MAGAZINE *would you believe it*   words get fainter *windows impossible* the cat
fallls WEAR DUNGAREES the air must be clear FAINT WORDS *ta ta* SPRING
YOU READ THE NEGATIVE RHYS *at church in april*   *go fool*   TOO MUCH
TWO MONTHS READ IN APRIL NOW DIFFICULT *at right angles* DONT
CHOOSE READ WITH SENSITIVE   NO WORDS red NOW flashes READ
WITH DUNGAREES DONT TRY THE IMPOSSIBLE IT HAPPENS IN APRIL
it wants it to reread April *is difficult* TAKE A DIGESTIVE GO TO SLEEP BEDS
KLEENEX MALCOLM COMING ITS TRUE THE WORDS DISAPPEAR
DONNIE KNOCK KNOCK   YOUR DRUNKING *dont mystify first question*
SECOND CHOICE says sleeping bag *who is first* BEST SECOND FIRST
CHOICE SHAME ON YOU BE CAREFUL *not consciously*
go to sleep

Sun be friend   *tomorrow night*
June 9 p3   NOW ITS APOSTROPHE
GO TO BED   YOU CAN SATISFY BED RHYS TOMORROW ITS CLASSIC
TOWN DONT WRITE ANYMORE
Monday   June 10   *Jana Friend peace*
YOU COULD BE HAPPIER YOU FEEL GUILTY large GO HOME PALE-
STINE GO TO BOSTON OBVIOUS EAT ENGLISH MUFFINS   YOU GET
ANGRIER YOIU COULD BE ANGRY *HAPPY* YOU COULD BE APRIL   BIG
HOUSE   READ APRIL ONE MORE STOP CALL JOHN MARRON YOU ARE A
BIG GIRL   .SEVEN READERSS BE EMBARRASSED IT'S THE RANDOM
HOUSE VOICE   YOU READ APRIL SEVEN TIMES YOU ARE BORED John
Marron was thinking of coming over no address THINK OF IT   VERY SUC-
CESSFUL PUBLISHING VENTURE he puts out a magazine *Bad Breath*   dont
drunk   YOU CALL RANDOM HOUSE MONDAY he READS   YOU OBEY
CHARLEMAGNE   TOOTS YOU ARE OBEDIENT John is coming over SOON
take the toothbrush out of it's mouth WASH UP ONE MORE WEEK   YOU
ARE AN EXCLUSIVE EAT LUNCH C ALL RANDOM HOUSE   IMMEDIATE-
LY STOMACH PUMP GET DRUNK YOU ARE DEFEATED no YOU FEEL
DEFEATED *you expected children* you get scared and hang up   GET DRUNK
you think something IT THINKS something DRUNK good is   YOU ALREADY
KNOW GET DRUNK YOU WONT BELIEVE IT   CALL RANDOM HOUSE
THE BOOK IS ADVERTISED SHE'S A GENIUS STOMACH PUMP You see
YOU'RE A GENIUS a second time you take CALCIUM ORGAS   NOW SEPT
MYSTERY NOVEL BIG LOVE TIRED THE CAT LEAVES the fire escape
window is open it has to rescue leave a message for Jim   yesterday DRINK IT
DRINKS DRUNK   THEY READ APRIL   it reads April early this morning
night and APRIL   READ APRIL   FRESH ROLLS MONDAY MORNING
TUESDAY   BARGAINS SUPPER the restaurant forgot to put its dinner on the
bill *you are overweight* on a budget YOU GET THIN C H I L D R E N
Charlemagne calls his animals children PHILOSOPHY John Marron leaves
THERE'S A HIERARCHY   Who's higher than IT?   JOHN OF ARC
BECAUSE   HEALING VICTORY He's interested in medicine, hear *tunafish*
eat some *don worry* Tibetan medicine NOS T lecture   CALL THE VOICE
YOU ARE PRECONSCIOUS   WEAR THE DUNGAREES   TIBETAN
MEDICINE you missed a lecture *medicine bile and angry flow* MIRIAM it calls
Tibetan office, no answer, Monastery coming back YOU CAN SEE HIM
WEDNESDAY YOU HOPE it's true   YOU HAVE A BACK PROBLEM   GO
TO A CHIROPRACTOR   *John Marron* calls dungarees blue jeans he says *Jasper*
an east coast term   SECONAL *John Perrault* SEE DANGER PRONOUN GET DRUNK it
had *drink* gin   change acidity   YOUR OWN FAULT CALL DR ____ Rhys
voice CONSCIOUS LEVEL says room at head level under light pull
                                              PERRAULT

73

Monday June 10 P 2

You wash YOU GET ANGRIER YOU ARE SAD AND DEPRESSED IT ISN't
BERNADETTE who is it you're IT IS happy *washing the dress* the blouse *the shirt*
YOU MEET NOA it is wide awake   IT DESCRIBES A NOVEL PEACE TODAY
YOU WHY IT IS THE LAUNDRY WOMAN *it finishes* washing the blouse it
remembers the lock to fix YOU TRY REMEMBER THINS SAYS THE DOOR
ONE MORE FUNNY PAGE   NEXT   YOU GET WEAKENED   BERNA-
DETTE CALLS NOT BEFORE 1 OCLOCK   ANUS PENIS   her words HER
POEM HER LIGHT YOU ARE BOLDER YOU CAN TAKE CALCIUM
ODIUM YOU ARE GIRL YOU MEET Pat calls JOB says phone Rhys needs one
YOU TRY ONE RING CALLED BERNADETTE ONE RING it said it hung up
IT CAME   PETER IS THERE dont believe in it   ALL DAY   DONT
LAUGH ENOUGH   LEWIS The Reader's *see danger*   Do You Believe in
Astrology HISTORY? HOW DO WE BATTLE WITH BRUPMS MORE
COFFEE   *Keep a funny poet in the house more compliments* YOU ARE
READY FOR A HOT DAY TOMORROW
MAKE EVERYBODY RHYS   THAT'S SUMMER
    everybody hates Rhys
   SHARON HAS A BIRTHDAY PARTY

                                        s   e   n
                                    a   o   u
                                  h   g
                                  t   h

                                                      o
                              e   f
                              g
                          a
                            p
                          s   i   h   t

LITTLE BOOK 111   SHEETS   Oct-Dec77

The useless
phrases
that have
INTRODUCTION

appeared in my
generation
TURNS PAGE

double indemnity
I am sure of itself
THE PLURAL PHRASES

I am settled
on a religious
principle
I AMS DEAD

THIS EMOTIONS
I am pregnant
this is not
a silly page

I thought she
was a woman too
Is anyone
included
　　HERE

wrinkles start
PHILOSOPHY
to appear
soon
TURNS PAGE

ugly *FOREHEAD*
old *UNDERLINES*
dear
underline

the INTERRUPTED

words I suppose its
words
I SUPPOSE

NEWS PAGE
try to look
silly once

CONTINUE

stupid
WRITE
ORANGE

write a book
now dear

S
 T
  E
   V
    E

he is LEAVING
sNEW YORK
SOON

STUPIDS OLD
IDIOT
SCRIPT

I wants forehead
scribbles a new
PSYCHIC
book from you
& remember
some   i c t s
      ioti lt
    id resu
      i r e
INSULTS
CHIRO
PRACTOR

useful *scripted*
things my
forehead says

to me
    I SAW THIS

I can be temporarily
funny all by
myself big dot
I FEEL LOUSY
    WHEN
    SILLY

when I'm unsociable with myself

    PAJAMAS

when it's 6:45
& I try ACCEPT
to sleep
  BIG DOT

nobody likes
this book.
  BIG DOT

I SHALL
WAIT
hear   jealous
me   I was thinking
I shall wait &
  then it appeared

for MUTTLEY

mehe
(I too speak)
HURRIED

temporarily
I SEE WORDS
ONS MY TOWEL

hear & see
I AMS SURROOM
          PRISED
me (early) this morning
                stupid
^I DESCRIBE

I SEE many DOCTORS
        MONDAY
I AM SURPRISED
AT MYSELF
OH HANNAH
GOOD THINKING

I REPEATS
I MAY REJOICE
hear JANUARY
      MUSELF

      I SEE
    SHELLEY
THANKSGIVING

      NIJOLE
w   t
  h   u
    a   o
      t   b
        a   a
          r   g
            e   i
                     k
                   n
              y i
                h
                o
                 u   t

      STUPID
      ANSWER

TURKEY HUGE
DINNER plus

**I DRINKS
PLENTY**

MARCH
you can always
overide your
fathers disciplinary
tactics

your mother is
NOTES
insistent
sometimes
SENTENCE

you can always
replace your
own mind
with a
MACHINE

I still have a
problem
submitting to
agriculture
HORMONES

I still have a
problem at
GOODRICH
night with
my *4-8*
sleeping
underlines interrup

**IONS
POSITIVE
BIG DOPE**

dont continue to
across screen
see **RACES
WITH THIS**

I ams a superior
person to myself
all the time
dont make any
more notes today
big stupid & silly
WHEN WRITTEN

try to**STOP WRITING**
substitute yourself
for another
person

I STOPPED

just a little
reward for your
patience
      PALESTINE
try to reverse
SUBSTITUTE
your sentence

structure
   **I READS BRUCE
A N D R E W S**

      **I
SHUTS
UP**

 DOPEY
you aren't even
a remarkable
writer **PERIOD**
yet
learn how Shelley
makes soup

**SATURDAY AFT
ERNOON**
just make it

a continual
project

"maybe they will
tell us so we
can warn the
world" Hannah
thats the chief
theory of *quote* TV
agriculture

are the planets
Mars
you are indis-
tinguishable
THIS BOOK
from science

are you on the
racing *saturday*
station stupid
 I AM
WRITING

you are almost
TELLS TRUTH
[a]SCIENTIFIC
MONSTER
scientist

you POLITICAL
are LOSING PAGES
making STATE
ments STUPID
and SILLY

Hannah this is
cheating a little
on you MARS
is on MY WORDS

TELEVISION

A CONTINUE
SENTENCE
little
            s e n t e n c e
                   e n t
                s
                   d
             e
           t
         l
       p
     m
   o
c

you must relax
a little in your
attitude toward
life SHELLEY
     SPEAKS

THATS DOPE
      Shelleys secret
I am on the po-
litical scene a
little stupid
ol silly AMEN

why are you
satisfied with
INSTRODUCTION
yourself
are you being
silly & stupid
     enough
THAS ENOUGH

its only later
that I discover
I
   KNOW PHYS
ICS something

IMPORTANT

I just dont do my
laundry often enough

I know nothing
Hannah I

STOP WRITING

JUST ENOUGH

COVER SIGNATURE

LITTLE BOOK 137   SILENCE   Mar 22 79

LEONARD
BOYS WE LEAVE
I DONST BELIEVE
HIM SOON
I have a terrible
time struggling
with it
MARY CROW DOG HITS HARD
SITS US IN SILENCE SISTER

I spoken to Mary
on the phone
and written it is
Hannah its very hard
FORGIVEN
to live with Indians

I said written it is
boys are we scolded
this is Leonards book
and it has pictures
in it
I wants to hear it
in my silence
stupid
       CHILDISH

Hannahs Ive
written it in
boys we love
sequence next
boys we are hard
it is written it in
last line next page

Hannahs we may
meet in May
sentence
ins silence
play it hard
thas enough

ENOUGH

Hannah it is
written it in
already it is
the boys know
that we
        AGAIN
I said scolded
JIMMIE

STOP THINKING OF IT
Hannah its the
sound first
its original
WE KNOW IT
before it happens
        3 YEARS MOST
stupid
HANNAH THATS CLEAR

Hannahs we must
learn it forever
it is written its
and we hides
        itself
Hannahs I have
learned too much
already HINT

I donst think it
really funny
that he FORGETS
Hannah skips poem
Hannahs handle
me directly
that means aloud
nos it doesnt
Hannahs it must
learn something else

Leonard is writing
it is in ENGLISH

Leonard is listening
to it
describe your scene
WITH THE BOYS
I SAID LEARN
we are speaking
of knowledge of course

HANNAH ITS SIMPLE
theres big trouble
in South Dakota
and we are forbidden
to enter here
unless he asks
me directly
THATS WHY We DELAY

Hannah its a
horrible sentence
not another year
in jail
we pray hard
Mary does
WE WINS

Leonard is speaking
to us in our
silence dear
stupid
ands we listen
Hannahs youre
VERY HUNGRY

Leonard is just
SILENCE
a little   like us
ANDS MEANS
we walk together
because of the
DONT SPEAK

POWER IS HIDDEN
SOMETIMES
thats Leonards theory

BECAUSE IT HURTS
ands in silence
TRUNGPA

We learn
Hannah its obvious
isnt it
DONST SPEAK
its our knowledge
correctly spelled
Hannah Im frightened of it
Hannah it is our
knowledge we
hold it in our silence

LEONARD IS VERY HARD ON US AGAIN
and we learn
SKIP 2 PAGES

Hannah that means we hold
our knowledge in common

thats Jimmie
he is very hard
Leonard SEQUENCE
is playing very
hard on us
MAKE IT OBVIOUS
and it hurts
Trungpa says

Hannah we cant
HEAVY PAGE
survive without
our secret
knowledge
Hannah handles
it in her silence
SO DOES LEONARD
forget the rest
THAS A HINT
GURUS SPEAK
LAST PAGE PLEASE

thats how Leonard
teaches us
NEXT PAGE PLEASE

TOOTS STOP WRITING IT IN

end of sentence
THIS BOOK IT IS
    ENDED
AND SPOKEN TO IT
    SIGNED
    LEONARD

SECOND POEM FOLLOWS THIS

SKIP TWO PAGES

HANNAHS HE SITS STILL THERE
THAT ENDS THIS POEM STUPID
AND CLOSED
SIGNED BOOK
SPEAKS TO MARY
SECOND POEM FOLLOWS

I SAID DONT WRITE
white writer writes
I didn't see it MARY
Leonard's life is
granted twice
AGAIN

MARY IS SPOKEN TO IN SILENCE STUPID
I MUST SEE IT BEFORE I WRITE IT
SECOND PAGE

MARY HAS PROOF
that Leonard leads
we are a Sioux writer
instead
Bow your head
& LISTEN
MARY SPEAKS

why white bread
MARY LISTENS
white writer instead
STAY INSIDE
AND PLAY
with the telephone
PLAY IT HARD
ON THE FARM
thats the game

IT SITS STILL FOR POWER

we play it backwards
dont tell the truth
sometimes
    I SAID IT
Mary IS AFRAID
OF HER LIFE
TWICE
that SKIPS PAGE

Mary is so scared
of her life she
wouldnt believe it
THAT SCARES IT
I'sm Leonards wife
in four years time
BEGINS AGAIN

stop writing it in
after dinner
Mary writes it in
I'sm Leonards wife
untils death
then we are through
with it
Trungpa is scared

I'sm still with
the Indians in
1984 the land
is granted free to them
I knows it before it happens it
Leonard speaks and closes this page

This is not a poem today I cannot write poems I can only write sentences The second sentence says that there are sins deadly to oneself and to others The third sentence says that some of these sins do include jealousy anger envy avarice pride because a person if she has spiritual power projects these qualities through her being and her work say writing and is imitated by others because of this power thus perpetuating what are called sins The third sentence which is here the fourth sentence was a long sentence and has to do with the need for work on the self The fifth sentence introduces one of Gandi's redefinitions of the seven deadly sins which deals with the political or work in the world The sixth sentence says that wealth even with work is no justification for keeping it all whether you work or inherit the obligation is to share until need is erased The seventh sentence quotes Gandi that pleasure without conscience is a sin but any act without conscience or consciousness is a sin and to close I have already committed seven sins seven sentences with meaning which I would prefer to destroy for a writer's goal of altering consciousness by means of disjunctive non-sequential techniques thus forwarding a consciousness which would eliminate sins however and whomever defined

Now I've got a feeling if you simply gather at the class of '50
Whether she was raped, deceived, bribed, seduced, persuaded
Some things I don't think I can do I end up doing
The original half-breeds, workers without patrimony
I thought you were a judge
A woman from the dominated class facing a man from the dominant class
We saved the government 85 million dollars
Oppression, repression, and discrimination
Why did I retire, it's a long story
A total disregard for the rights of the poor
Anna Marie had 13 children
Political, social and economic discrimination
Mary had 9, youngest 17
Guatemalan women have been relegated to the realm of the household and to
         domestic labor
I taught for a year at Carol Center
Upper class has relied fundamentally on machismo
We have six bedrooms
They are paid lower wages than the men
Our parents were getting older so we did add on in a fashion
Women constitute only 13.7 of the employed
Thats very nice. I wonder if maybe they make extra keys
Girls constitute 12.6 percent of the juvenile labor force (children from 10 to14)
Kitsy, are you still in the diplomatic corp?
Eighty per cent of Guatemalan households lack drinking water, electicity
She was a very nice mother, very capable
Laundry is done at the river
She had to raise five children by herself
Minimal health care services scarcely exist
She's really into the woman's movement
In thirty years, in spite of "modern" legislation, only five women have been elected
         to congress
I don't have a model for being a woman who was still active

Peasant women attend to household chores and to their children, but they also
work in agricultural activities, later selling the harvested produce
Who's the girl, the feminist with the long hair?
The market women are denied the right to organize
My mother kinda got fixed into a little pattern
Annual migration of indigenous peasants from the highlands to the large southern
coastal plantations to pick cotton, coffee, beans and sugar cane
My sisters are all a fair bit older than I
Must carry her youngest child on her back while working in the fields
We all have changed a little bit
The work-day begins at 4:00 in the morning and doesn't end until 9:00 or 10:00
at night
We knew exactly what we should do, get married
When her work is weighed or measured by the foreman she is cheated shamelessly
We produced exactly the same number as the national average
Not provided with any protection against the toxic effects of the insecticides
Fifty-five masters degrees
For housing they are herded into barracks too filthy for human occupation
We're poised at this historically important point
Indian women who work as domestics are obliged little by little to adopt ladino
ways and customs
If you can feed something like that into the questionnaire
Women are also exploited sexually by factory owners and foremen
Grading English compositions for twenty years gets to you
Those women who participate in an organizing drive are fired
I have a two year old grand-daughter I've been baby sitting for
Any woman fired can easily be replaced from among the pool of thousands of
unemployed women
We've tried younger volunteers
Many indigenous women survive in the cities by making tortillas
I married and had four children and did all of that
75,000 teachers are unemployed, most of them women
We had one young man who recently left the seminary
Indigenous teachers must very often pretend to be ladinos
My husband was alcoholic
Women of the rural areas, both Indians and ladinos, have joined the struggle

I had power in the field of civil rights

She led hundreds of peasants in a struggle for land

We'd better grab two quick minutes for class business

More than one hundred peasants from Panzos were murdered on May 20, 1976

What are your perspectives on Radcliffe at this moment

A war of extermination, primarily waged against the Indian people

My father could still recognize me

In February, 1980, over 76,000 semi-proletarian agricultural workers went
      on strike

This woman wanted to shut off her husband's feeding tube

Leadership of the Committee for Peasant Unity (CUC)

My mother brought us up

Involvement in the struggle has meant confrontation with society, culture,
      and family

Even if you work with a computer, doing your own programming

The needs of the revolution have opened the eyes of the people

Look at Russia and its health care delivery situation

Cultural changes in the attitudes toward women are required

The Russians are a lot smarter

Many women companeras have been obliged to sever ties with their families

And the British system, if you look at it cosmically

Entire families are being drawn into the revolution

We have the resources to have a superb health care system

Oppressed by North American imperialism, oppressed as women, women are the
      slaves of slaves

Health care is a business

The army kidnapped or murdered their husbands

There should be something more human about it

Women have assumed responsibility for caring for children not their own

Today with jet planes filling the skies

Women participate along with men in village meetings

If we have any vision of a flourishing economic world

They do guard duty and set up traps for the enemy

When we were still emerging as a world power

Sabotage measures digging trenches; they devise warning signals and flight plans
      for the villagers

Our own economic policies

Women work in literacy campaigns among women

We can again take the offense seeking a global market

They care for the gunshot wounds of the villagers

In the aftermath of the last great economic crises

Hundreds of women—with infants on their backs—sabotaged several miles of
        the highway

But today we have a new generation

Definitive liberation from U.S. imperialism and local dictatorships

Confidence is the most precious asset

She helped educate the other women and children

To exercise strong supervision and regulation

In meetings with the women she would act as translator

The lessons of financial crises

There is a lot that women can do in this struggle, which is everyone's struggle

A strong sense of business integrity

She saw members of her family murdered by the army

To protect the public at large

She became a leader of the popular movement

My own alma-mater since the days of President Wilson

I started working for a living when I was eight years old, on the plantations

Have shared that tradition

I could no longer bear the expression of pain on my mother's face. She was
        always exhausted

In the end it's a matter of respect

My wage, when I started, was twenty cents a day

The responsibility of government

When I was eleven, two of my little brothers died on the plantation from
        malnutrition and sickness

Bettering the lot of our communities

We used to get up at three in the morning

Stability and continuity

For breakfast we had tortillas with salt

Larger national purposes

Customs dont permit a young girl to walk alone

My concern is with economics as a responsibility of government

For us, the earth is sacred

We will succeed

When I was fifteen, in 1973, my father was arrested for the first time

They can call on a lot of PHD's for technical abilities

It was all the rich who persecuted us campesinos

Let's make the most of them

He suffered a lot of pain and could not work in the fields

For all those women throughout the world who are torn by political and economic
    revolution and by attacks against home and family

We taught the children how to guard the road during the day

A truly liberating education

Soon afterward my father was killed...burned alive inside the embassy

With an appreciation of the humanistic worlds

My mother died three months later. The military chief raped her and tortured her
    like they did to my brother

I am very proud of the history of Radcliffe

They placed her under a tree and her body became infested with worms

Radcliffe has done so well, in fact

The troops stayed until the vultures and dogs ate her

Most Radcliffe women today

The only thing I can do is struggle, to practice that violence which I learned in
    the Bible

The studies to improve women's higher education

The rich and the army say that all of us Indian people are communists.... So for
    our own safety...we have stopped wearing our Indian dress

We are grateful to you alumnae

In 1970-71, when thousands of workers and peasants "disappeared" political
    assasination became a daily reality

It was an intimidating institution

The struggles waged by the teachers movement are intense

An outward veneer of academic success

Teenagers, as well as mature and even elderly women, take part in demonstrations

A lot more self assurance than I had at first perceived

The association of Families of the Disappeared was able to operate until 1974,
    when its legal advisor was assassinated

I redirected my career

Along with disappearances, kidnappings and torture, women (including girls of 14
     and 15 and even elderly women) are raped

We are now reaching the point in our lives

Not only are women raped, they are also blinded

A woman should not draw attention to her achievement

Yet another form of torture is the firing of machine-gun rounds into the vagina

Those of us who pursued active careers

I know that a disappearance means almost certain death

In contrast we have been freed

People turn up badly tortured. They obviously suffered terribly before they died

It is clear that young women today

It was engineered, as we all know, by the CIA. I mean the CIA says this quite
     frankly

They are making far fewer early marriages

Peasant self-defense league—the CUC or Committee for Peasant Unity

The super woman approach places a tremendous burden

How old was she when she disappeared? Sixty five

We would like to be later-day Renaissance women

Indians in Guatemala are among the most down-trodden human groups

To work for the virtual irradication of tuberculosis

The supposedly democratic elections are nothing but an incredible farce.
     You have nothing except the right and the far right

I had such a wonderful life

We do not want American military aid to Guatemala renewed

This award is really a tribute

The CUC has local committees in small settlements, hamlets, villages and even in
     the city where there are poor people

And was I think a great teacher

We women participate equally with men

Learning was a wonderful experience

Celia, the youngest, who is only 13

I received a wonderful background

4,000 peasants participated with us demanding this wage. Many of them were
     assasinated, kidnapped and threatened

He taught me what research was all about

How long did the strike last? It lasted a month or more

We're coming to the close of a wonderful afternoon

plurals describe multisquarrelavoided brothertwo time   he can

imagine this describes   show his mistakes   even   smyname   know

concrete walks made two comments whistfully OPEN i   a m s

t e a c h i n g at suds   the clear often describe   t h e   life of the

city   HANNAH THATS A VERY REAL COMMENTnot obliged speaking on the page

     and indent altruist put the words down a taste of following

instructions paper all sentences begin   that was hard we portola

are here   we the people   thinnest   did you measure theplace 1/2 INCH it

i own mine   why by the   all the colors disguise weagree somone

is overrigged & line heavy with water, but throughout the yard the

greens deepen. Iron Hannah I dont think any more either   sum   at

the corner whose cutouts as yours that means   distance you were

working and I describe the city although   somealachite ors

demand underground some as we read   some joke   pints & quartz adverbs
                     coal
are unlimited andwe quarrel/I am leaving the ground   he describes

frp, winter memory sometime.   Scratch same simile above   dont

               use it   The dress hurts
               language like like out thus
a sudden change   describe variable description   well we hints

it isn't always the best CONCRETE SIDEWALK   thing to do because

someone walks   or they turn it away   it is only some beginners

trick ourselves medicine   Hannah that means you were like Leonard

Crow Dog a little how much working

you notice the differences because you are entirely conscious

asmost children in Europe could detail the why we are open   was

anyway it sometime without people in it garbage hurts us over

the counter you're answering his questions stupid sis it winter

OK youre in it   with a sweater comfor on   five days   quote

Hannah that is Babytears and ---- and carrots   unhistorical process
writing begin with blank make sure it is alternate clear away the
postage dishes comment Hannah thats the run on complete abstinence
sentence & Charles cant copy your but bruce complete can in the
explain I am the only one recorded sentence get charles at the
office official in again sowat my darling the sheet is clear
but isnt two words offer offering babycarrots and unend like me
separate
quote the book Babytears & seen words are underlined & some carrots
Hannah he has possessions on his mind and you dont unless weare
working in the field why buy atall the eating and carrots sometime
plural sometime mother likes a period. like in the spring this
season ground soft will grow upstate farmers choice andthen eat
Hannah thats plural we dont upset the applecart or the farmers
choice and period mother unless we quiet down we are all spoken
this period. Hannah just describe the description and words begin
the in the book buzz of some similar flies fills the yard, cats
I am quoting him notteaching inthis book andclear himself stretch
and period calm water speaks. the next page mother underlines all
spoken teach allwater is clear underground if not polluted upstream
by the enemy orthe client historical where is the water clear inthis
land second sentence iquote Bougainvillaea & same babytears some
ampersand sign which i dont because the illiterate cant read the
money it looks like the money sign some Indians hurt if you arent
living with it the signals are across on the street andiquote inthe
fog fogdrifts limit some sense distance and some microscopic rain
like thought second choice and end godforgiven eliminate those whorls
called flips like ( ). and now we come to the last sentence mother
rules the short sentence behind andwhich allenter the short sentence
is inclined to get it overwith the business problem which i did

eating the carrots which is business and which is allsplay   dont
destroy the form sentence just awkward bullrshes plain i want him
to working separate his cats disappearance verbs so hewill learn
altruistic prose like clear theend working at the mothers knee
and so russell means signs wednesday alltrue thispiece andso ilost
a bluebook
and the sentence please we all are working inthe church scene
mother would comment on the end of the short sentence and it
finishes it two pages

JULY 21 TUES

WHAT IS THE STYLE PREVALENT IN OUR OWN AGE CLASSICAL

I dont mind the name calling me up again but he wont do

it if I only
       TRANSPARENCE
wait only   he is retired for the summer if its only
                  SENTENCE
somename is back very happily in her OWN subject

preschool children are INHIBITED by small town occurances

first somename would talk be happily SUNDAY in it READING IS

OVER   some Indians are in with it the STAYED ON   with it

the land REVOLUTION sis I stayed with the
                EMPORIUM
style CONFLICT IN THE MAY OVER WHICH READING
                   CANCELLED
I must the May poetry project style group in it   NO ONE

UNDERSTANDS ME
        READING
SIMPLY OR THE WOMAN FAST HAS IT   UNEMOTIONAL   WHAT IF

THE STRIKE IS OVER   WRITE darling A SMALL POSTCARD SEPT

ARRIVES TO BE CERTAIN I MUST CALL HIM WEDNESDAY BACK   BUT

DONT MEET THURSDAY NIGHT   Im over fifty
                  AND DONT BECAUSE IN IT
sis kill the rura business problem   name on the phone

LET HIM KNOW ME in it PROBLEM SKIP THE NAME PAGE

JULY 23 THURS

my name   COURTHOUSE we are OIL strucking oil the island off read

some science interviews   and pen   of course the old government

we live poor of completed course   SIS KID THE HELL ENGLAND OUT OF

the Irish soname OH OL SCHOOL TIES ARE HARV   EMBELLISHED OR WRONG

GET RID OF THE OLD SCHOOL TIES

HELP REKA IN THE KITCHEN   SIS KIND   ·

AND DONT HOLD ONTO YOUR MOTHER FIRST

SIS ITS BICYCLE TIME AT 10 OCLOCK

I pencil READ past A BOOK autography there is some sacrifice kid

sentimental in staying DARLING in your sentence completed mothers

INDOLENT house   sis its just a small sacrifice to write postal

strike LEARN WHAT THE WORKERS about it   thats all and sentence
                            FEEL
why did I the me destroy the sentence blurp   because the rhyme the

mind responds thinks quicker THAN WE SPEAK and answers below the
                    OR SEE WE IT THE WORDS
line itself on the page   Hannah people

stink with riches dont care the bums on the stre survival et are

working like us APPEAR Hannah thats ok   HOUT   HURRY   SYNTAX
                                        w I

OR COMPLETE some prevPRINTious THOUGHT OR INCLUDE INSTRUCTIONS

LIKE CAPS we win Hannah please dont print some sequence it anymore

and period and quit some

JULY 28 THE QUEEN

say its tues   THE MIND efficient method seen screen is

and the   not the method most often used to complete

wedding   QUEEN OPP this phrase is the wedding official

is official   YOU can swim on Friday morning AND THEN WRITE

WEDNESDAY that the official code is subversive against

dont mention the queen's name   the why tears grain I dont

tomorrow   want to be a PICTURE wedding OFFICIAL picture

and let me   because I was very scared   sis dont write

be solo   any more about Queen opp's picture   the

interrupted   official wedding SCOLD ONS THE FLOOR SOMETIME

THE QUEEN OPP   picture thats period my name she punctuates

please   wasnt she a lovely young across the street
all ends
                doesnt HURT girl once

at the library   sis its all her the queen opp BABIES own

fault sis if she likes children she will orphans be a EDUCATED

very great bossy queen   she must save the lives of 100 children

PRAISE a day and learn sis it was the official wedding portrait

and the green gown wasnt her babies own sis she has several

wardrobes full of old WOMANS clean it up clothes W A R D R O B E

in the closet   I was warning signals instantly on the red cross she is definitely a babies mother   six ONLY FOUR children

cant you see the she adopts one   royal family ORGANIC populating

she hints the world and some other WORLD ORGANIZATION magazine

if she were depressed ARM ACUPUNTURE she wouldnt cry about

RIGHT HAND it   so its my aunt absolutely DONT SIT ON THE FLOOR

covered   my name the whole point is the royal family is getting

or having its   its picture HOME taken   if it was a very

serious movie I couldnt stay late unless it was well liked

by both   sis its ok not to we quarrel finish PUBLICATION

writing this article   sis dont drink with them on the floor

and say goodnight say goodnight and omit little marie's

name   SAME CLOSED and some period dots   and the conclusion

is mother understands   blue sweater   the BLACK PANTS philosophy

sis dont match the pants to the jacket   thats all and oh so

my name dont point   circles   some closed   itinerant sis

its OK closed the morning book and the queen opp's wedding

some   if it was a popular model I would write behind a lot

and it disnt or public EITHER or public or so   sis its all

about writing a great big writing novel   sis it doesnt square

either   mother didnt like the sweater at first because it was a hippie's selection and very expensi_{lambswool}ve one   and

dont buy store or store who are electrically involved in

spreading _{nuclear} prosperity and the image for centuries
well thats an table argu sis dont hint any

BIG SWEATER remains   and this closed book is OK and remember
more big bombs nuclear we are optimal understanding much it

store   sis its not a stupid novel to write neighbor anyway
better if we die for it sometime and I dont work otherwise

or across the street   sis if its only work I wouldnt mind
I can feel more without the streets hyer arch y or across

sis its a funny book if you like writing a novel and cant
the street it hurts i like the mens welfare shelter bums any_w
 WITHSTAN stand with it name my name its just a lot of ^{a}y
^{h}_an honest theyre across the street liquor and i dont drink or

publicity   my name they guess if only working you separate
catch cold or bed or sometime anymore withit like

bedrooms could walk across the street more often   blue

across the UPPER page   I didnt finish my sentence MISGIVINGS

at spell   the last   I can be PROMISE forgiven Mon in et al
                i think sometimes
etc included and spelled mistaken correctly   ture   I SOMETIMES

WONDER IF writing IT IS period TRUE   PERIOD   AUGUST because

of the many predictions   I have made this continued

please journey at last this is home period style   sis if

REKA I get my period twice Aug again I will SQUAWK and killing me

SO ITS AN wed WEDDING important line   sis its OK to go DRAWER

leave it open to sleep on the wedding day   with they have four

hours days months   privacy it all   and included make sure the

children business is offset and publishing incl

AUG 13

So you know me also anybody wrist taped   so I was written

it in again so I was also August only   I ALSO WRITTEN   I

was also else   I was different only   Saturday   I

WAS DRINKIN   I was drunken   only 2 martinis   I was lonely

edge   I was written in   spoiled   in my arithmetic class

spelled   CORRECT ly   I was also two x two   I was also any

person   I was spoiled stupid   I can eaten by dinner   I was

frightened by them downstairs   I like socialism   I like

brown pen but I dont own any   I was boughten by lipstick

I was offering a sale   I was difflong list erent   I was

anybody else   I was   terrific   I also drunken too   I was

insolete   I was obtained   I was original copy   I was

insistant   who am signa   I   ture   I was also indifferent

to this   upper lower case   indifferent   by some words

I was also   written July in Sept   I was afraid to leave

immediately on signal   and dont obey instructions   this

page please us

I WAS WRITTEN

I was also anybody social systems work telepathically   so

its I'M giving instructions silent when I read before a large

crowd apostrophe   I was weakened early   I was in bad state

memory   by the power also   by also this   current   incorrect
wickened

so some pen pleases us   to us written   so this is ending

MOTHER IS DOWNSTAIRS   DRUNK   is also downstairs in WRITTEN
                    also

language   is holistic written   is knowledge   self absorbed

by obedient children   is also training   inefficiency   I
                              supper

was   also absorbed   sis its killing them   I was also

absorbed inefficiency   so it is written theory in   someone
                              turkey

else has absorbed our potassium pie   our leader has a finger

in it   so he scolded us   for scolded people lie and   breakdown

under interference or scolded
                    OR SCOLDED

            I   WAS   SCOLDED

I didnt hurt Lewis anybody and insurance

introduction as class i see words between lines   on sign

Alex Hladky is dead, burial, movement leader as white as

could be as seen I words, sojourn PERIO

the following is ALL SEEN AS WORDS BEFORE i

write mother IT DOWN IN THE BOOK   AS CLASS

the I Ching THROW said 16 the number Enthusiasm

S U I C Iin a carD E following the change 17 on

Alex Hladky's death late fall 1982   I was promised

to him just a little bit everyone all

otherwise the piece as usual was following orders en

titled BY MYSELF IN SEEN WORDS the number

sixteen sentences seen this summer 82 THE SAME

AS ABOVE period

Sixteen period dots are seen at the end of this
sequence sentence and you should

W R I T E I T D O W N

G R A N D M O T H E R

since nearly ago since my fathers died was I
written pen in sack   well we pass an awkward
sentence in style   THIS TIME I READ IT MY TIME
ON THE ^{oct} LIST   how many trips to Prov still
left   only one awkward situation   we GIFTS
DANNY   my nephew   well my father died of jealousy
perhaps in his late old age of figures

    why we are written

    goldfine but he

    played stock

    market toots and

    apparel industries

within it was written we are enlarged pancreas
boys died   Charles didnt   well the stock market
industries are up and he died already plus period
which I dont have any from my sunburn and my nice hat
which is brim oldwritten some other style   some style
written   my mother died when she was a very young
girl like 90 go hunt as some bears and feel it
END OF SENTENCE

I spoke of the money problem we tighten last loop

our belts   once or twice   and it cost us even

hundred dollars to come here   why written because

I seen it alway   without periods   mother thinks you're

hunting in good style finish para way out west my

grandmother gertrude include letter same

DEAR CHARLES WAS READING IN IT WITH IT ALL
                                                    THIS
PRINT THE TIME PLEASE EN SAY LITTLE BO THAT
                                                    WAS
YOURS please return immediately by sending some

sentence structure through the mail

                        SOMEONE ELSE

WROTE BELOW THE

                        LI

NE

                        WAS IT YO

we continued on the line sentence CLOSE VERY CAREFUL

WRITER   did you thank him for sending you publish

write Kathy the little book   Hannah its the wrong

notebook for this some letter spacing   teach Susan

TECHNIQUE BUY scratch another TELL GEORGE if

I WANT POST CARD pray very little hard during sundance

Aug 4-5 my teacher tells Hannah thats how Satchidananda

speaks you to telling truth keep this Barrett copy

I am learning please enclose this letter with this

answer the mail below the line competent

CHARLES

criminal

I was working

INSTRUCTIONS I was teaching him

three more years of this and I suffer   Oct church

reading

with him in it
secluse

like Susan

copy this letter on letter paper   sis he's born

twice again   boy is he scared this instructions

include July 8   send some sundance money just a

little to them eliminate address this let him Rosebud

decide address   no one else would dream of entering

this wisdom in it of letter form   we are reading

isolated   Is met Tom just once and he didnt like

it when spoiled very much either   tell Susan I love

her anyway

second letter

Hannah thats all I ever say it   Indians who come to

the reservation them we are the political leaders are

hidden until Sundance Wednes time   where we hid

you once from the boys   well that old Crowdog

means Bill Means is working with us again plenty

and spot.   keep this in a box letter alway

Susan cries she speaks grandmoth

who is teaching us all again through her mind only

like me also   put your name under the sign

                                Han whoever you are

we are the Indian teachers also BORN   as was

Christian thats what they say our Lord   over the

land battle we Charles is in tears fought

                                      B E C A U S E

I was teaching with him   sis I fought over the land

battle with them and they cried a little bit over

the money   CHAR returns two splits

                G R A N D M O T H

in three or four weeks I will be with yours   in a

little mailbox   I send some pills   you must know

why I am heal   the most important letter was in

our civilization direct BYS THE MAIL

WELL I CLOSE THIS LETTER Bruce does   Childress

                                    BY MY OWN

already known hand Steve and wife Diana Childress

Ron Sillimannother letter

well I with it   nobody else reads this letter but

Reka Marks and hang it on the wall   mother picture
lost dear   last line   even Bernadette cried last
winter when I was lonely just a little bit   boy is
that I mean grandmother a forget this line   send
George a copy   please mother thinks I shouldnt write
this letter to anybody

send Canada mag soon I was with dont mention names in
it a little bit but he declined THAT MEANS MONEY
sis it means I was declined political to be a
little reader page get me over Indians   tell
George its a political freedom issue and I dont get
it in wherewho   scared a little my teeths   my
mother sudden realization   George calls   where is
the hippie money   we bought em out bruce problem
SIS WE JUST JUMPED ON THE TRAIN AND ride away HID
be very careful Indian with your letter   I send
you postcard now   have you ever we feel stood   be
with the land   silent   before a great stone
sis its a great big change   Rosmarie comes for you
if you lead them Charles silent without
talking brothers   mother would scratch out her
religious ceremony last name forever celibate
sis I choose to remain celibate for a life when
I return 86   plenty of company   sis slightly

dangerous to know them Crow Dogs   so many people
wonder   why I wrote never this letter   what is the
great spiritual achievement TO THIS HOLY LAND RE
        T U R N
                        or I will die
before your keep me alive mother
                              64 I beg
Hannah thats when I say money gone   I'm starving
thats when the money from the land is gone   I mean
the house   sis thats letter gone OK with us date
please July 29 very late 82 the year before my
mother dies because she was sleep   Hannah we
Leonard Crow Dog remem publish this letter bered
it in twice
                        Hana Weiner
                        place
                        my mothers home
                        39 Emeline St
                        Prov R I 02906
        U N T I L S   N O V E M B
mother would close this letter and call her name
my house is open childless to them when they
return NYC
Because I was with Indians last page of letter I
am remembered
                        also date 8/17/82

way out west my grandmother gertrude is waiting
for me to write her a letter put it down   well we
written it is   central intelligence agency is also
official agency way out west   not too many whites
this year also firmteen   we all through   well we
written it is

ON THE TRAIN

as always   and conclude
popular Providence   how much did your string sweater
cost you sister $15 no the new one   well save it
how much did your white shorts cost you sister
I was borrowed it name   so nothing and three years
old send them back to the New York City   I borrowed
Billie   why we are old grandmother   to see visions
in the sky   I play Sundance record   I only poet
on the scene reading with it   I wear dress

       skip name

I was written it is   oh my cold short is my
grandmother's house in Feb   why I am ill   in the
cold Feb snow   why didnt Providence we sit still
mother thinks its the longest year of her life
ahead of her   come home early Feb until March
skip scene write me

GRANDMOTHER

cold house down thas enough   come home hang up yr
coat be stand

oh we have breakfast so many times   sis its an
old winter coat she wants   LIVE POOR for the Indians
who are not by me forgotten   write her a great big
goddam line in this and settle mother is pleased
problem
                    S A T C H I D A N A N D A
Conn on the line please   dial with your little
finger you're OK   have you ever heard of the
grandmother's poem
        I T   W A S   W R I T T E N   I T   I S
                    A P P L E
every line gets written in the bathroom sink
sis I act like efficient secretary   until the
fast comes out we are unbeloved   I also was
protein conscious like fish
                        W E
                    S M E L L
so very street lights are in it   it takes three
centuries to understand what was written because
I feel with it known   it was my grandmother's
poem and she remembered it in when I the type   sis

very high energy field was also with it Indians are
ver scared with their life pray for Vernon who cares
at the city   only two people know I'm dying of
leprosy CALL THE BEGGARS a very powerful woman
writer writes it down   FEEL COMFORTABLE for at
least one week   sis its OK you have written it is
include Berna's name   once a week I take myself through
a trial course to see if I can jump high enough
write it down and separate the sentences   six
periods plus

R O M E O

periods are being written down by me in this
CIGARETTE little black book and you wont believe
it plus Romeo and Juliet cant be confirmed

I   L I K E

in two or three LIVE LONGER years no money problems
HERE   yes my mother says grandmother so long to be
with it

C H A R L E M A G
L O V E R

to be   in three years I will remember this   I am
alone   I WAS WISHED UPON IT BY THE ME   I still
drink coffee lover I WANT MY LOVER two weeks BACK
FRIDAY ASK HIM FOR THE BOOK BEFORE HE
                    WEEKEND   CRIES

THAT I AM

TOM

breakdown

under stress OLDER complete page

in exactly when mother is ill   three years I shall

be BURIED dead   so what if I dont care

MOTHER

Hannah old Mrs Crow Dog will ill pneumonia   write

it down   so I believe my mother first   sis if she

shakes the wind she will die   down in the teepee

I become clear over her head   she sits still with

it either   no the mailbox just get a large note

SCRIBBLE

book and type   by my will Disabill secure AND PARAGRA

in my grandmother's house many years I furniture

have past dont steal the clothes life   plus she

sees me in her mind with my mother sit close and dont

TUESDAY

touch her across the breast   sis it means I dont

cold shoulder her   I think Betty she has cancer but

they diet cant find it right now   some CALCIUM deposits

IN THE BRAIN

I moved the furniture

cold house

in the winter

why be celibate

OPEN   WINDOWS

my little mouse is mother is crying a little

for me upstairs writing   sis its so sure to be OK

with the little house me my mothers house   she has

a cold house in wintertime   fix it up   only

one woman knows

WRITING

my mother is   so I know what is grandmother's house

sis she fixes table it up exactly like close mine

wrong with her by the little table   sis I need food

COLD
H
O
U
S
E

from refrigerator   sis she ill november   sis she

cries when she hears I'm writing about her endless

knows exactly whats wrong with me by the little close

by windows pills   dont live in a cold shoulder

house   plus I eat cold

WINTE

food   plus extra allowance   I am pouring rain Sundance

until last line below the skip two

118

line Sunday   the people come to us the people George

thinks write proofs in the mail it down   in Leonard's

voice 3 years I will cut this tape

I   W A S   W O R K I N G

S I N G L E

I will have told everyone what's wrong with them

s a t u r d a y   n i g h t   a list

go shopping

my right shoulder strap

old coat plus clean

reline

buy yourself dress

clean white pants

redry in sun

you just like me

G R A N D M O T H E R

sits still with Hopi reunion
we are very glad
during Sundance written

that you obey us

H O U S E

protects me all next winter when my mother's

clothes fails   that means we poor   um beg

sudden chills

A VERY GOOD PARENT SITS OUTSIDE let her buy me

clothes   why old Henry likes us   we hang up

the phone   funny girl over the page   Hannah it

sounds to George like a ritual best guide please

end   we argue a little   sis its just a little

confined selfish of you to read letter   end this

page

well I monday suffered

G R A N D M O T H E R S

B O O K

a little for it   sis if its written it is it will

be shown WRITE DOWN some weeks ago I pulmonary

pneumonia had twist headaches relax the wrist   sis

dont kid yourself   youre a great big writer with

Russian influence

E M B A S S Y

Hannah they think youre a very cute girl thats all

relax   show grandmother who can read Jan this

small print   two readings anyway   plus Tues bitter

because I see it   Guess what the Russians say

I didnt like it the first surprise time I saw itperiod close

I   S A W   W R O N G

Rosmarie Waldrop indent form the rhyme   the

broken promises of treaty should be beginners lessons

go eiffel tower seen in picture form easy on them trips
them we are the Indians forgiven who is like me seen
on slant anyway

H A N A   G U E S S   W H Y

Hannah one sip put it in that you drank tasted a little
coffee saw oh juice   oh boy meets   one line below
Hannah thats little book not mention names   significant
prose   write some lyrics for

BLUE BOOK

us baby and

SIGN OFF

we'll sung ya

SEEN Introduction

Before the Code Poems please I was just short page an ordinary writer no instructions and one book was published. The Code Poems were performance pieces using two figures and flags and were found material based on the International Code of Signals for Ships at Sea.

Before I was introduced to myself. The book was published last. Last sentence. Before I became my clairvoyant writer myself.

That's the belief introduction

SHORT PAGE

Someone else would get hysterical.

And words began to be seen in August then begin 1972 almost   after seeing images and energy fields since January 1970 some inclusion and writing journals some unpublished.

Then we began to see words as aforesaid and write some journal its all enclosed   I still do
        All the introduction is seen.

Establish yourself. Some writers are very difficult but I seem unusually   Hannah I have to offer myself   Read one line at a time it pleases you.

Some introduction fin   Have some courage put it plain the introduction one page seen and I am almost

INTERVIEWED

The Development of the Sentence in My Work in SEEN WORDS

When the words first began to appear in August 1972, they appeared singly. The first word, WRONG, appeared about an inch long, neatly printed at a 45 degree angle to my pant leg. Later words appeared in two word phrases some of which, as NO-ALONE, I did not understand (Early Journals, 1972, unpublished). In my naive (or natural form) desire for completion I would cry "where is my T—is it the phrases 'not alone' that is meant" and why cannot I or it or the spirits that I then sometimes thought it was, speak English. The phrase developed but remained a phrase right up through the Clairvoyant Journal (1974, Angel Hair 1978). In April sometime I think I got down on my knees and begged or prayed, please let me see a complete sentence. On April 15th I did see one, printed in small letters along the edge of my kitchen table that had come to me from Lenny Neufeld via Jerry Rothenberg. It said, "YOU WONT BE ANY HAPPIER."

Having achieved this wonderful goal (my mind could spak English, after all, I could) I then proceeded to discontinue the sentence. The words appeared too fast and interrupted themselves. The (my) natural desire for closure was defeated by the more important mind—or poetic—form. I was happy though, complete thought.

Lyn Hejinian says in "The Rejection of Closure," (Poetics Journal #4 May 1984 Women & Language) "...a natural response toward closure, whether defensive or comprehensive, and the equal impulse toward a necessarily open-ended and continuous response to what's perceived as the 'world,' unfinished and incomplete." She also states "Form is not a fixture but an activity" which was certainly true of both the Clairvoyant Journal and Little Books / Indians (ROOF).

Long sentences in Little Books / Indians were interrupted often by capital letter words as well as regular lower case in which the book was mostly written. Many of these words and sentences were completed if my memory could hold onto the long seen phrase which was interrupted by newer seen phrases. The complete sentence or thought then depended on my memory and if (as in the poem "Page 2 Numbered") I had smoked some marijuana the memory was elusive and hard to hang onto.

    Little Book 129   Page 2 Numbered   Oct 26 78"

    Here comes a sentence S T R U C T UbruceR E
    that DONT WRITE
    I must make
    a con MY BOOKS
       describe a story
    the bell rings

twice & Bernadette's voice I run downdont skip Charles
I THOUGHT IT WAS MY BOOKS I JUST UPSIDE RAN
and nobody stands
Hannah its so
simple it hurts same line you
STAND IN YOUR SILENCE dont skip

But I dont remember what I said
the sequence stands
typical sentencesame line struct
                    YOU

and

sentence structure some exclamation MY SAME SENTENCE
Danny returns
and it has an ending
giving away our
SILENCE
CRAZY DONT SKIP GIRL what was I saying
an hour ago what I was
reverse sentence
SILENCEsome pages

Danny reports it on you Hannah dont speak overline
its just the sentence
PUNCTUATION
I canst remember sentence I folded my pages
AN HOUR AGO

In "hiding JAPAN" another long sentence poem, I had not smoked any grass and the
interruptions were part of the original seen line, not something that intervened after I had
started to write the first part of the line.

Little Book 134   hiding JAPAN   Dec 19 78

WAIST my rings hurt something else is Jimmie wrong INSIDE
    RUSSELL MEANS uptown LIGHT I dont know what
    PERIOD dont finish sentence please
See what Jimmie SORRY ABOUT THIS really phrase continues
    carry your books in a sack stupid MEANS TO APRIL
    THAS FINISHED
RUSSELL MEANS ME
HANNAHS I started my sentences again SKIPS A PAGE
Donst date he feels it Jimmie has made the final decision of dont
    continue with this dont speaks of this his POOR entire
    next page GURUS
Dont be so stupid life sentence structure please that was because
of SAME PRICE me I CANST WRITE IT IN
Jimmie has decided to become SENTENCE STRUCTURE
    SAME AS ME   LONG LINES
Jimmie sentence structure WRITE IN JOY APRIL has decided
    to become Hannah finishes her sentences WE WEAKEN
    EASILY

As for other drugs, I don't take any (except some Peyote in ceremony which I don't write on, but Peyote brings picture visions, not words).

Drinking, however, when I am seeing words, will completely mix me up and force a memory loss so that what I write is usually edited out. The disjunctions are out of hand and not interesting to me—too much out of control and I cannot complete the interrupted line. Perhaps I just get silly. Some drunk (seen) some perhaps (seen) some talk is in perhaps some (seen).

This summer 84, however, not seeing words, I wrote drunk very long very ordinary prose lines—also not interesting to me and also silly. Coffee is fine.

Spoke (Sun & Moon) was written differently. The words appeared on my forehead in groups short enough for me to remember and write them down and the continuation or interrruptions were included in this word-group seeing. This is true even though the style varies from a journalistic technique (June & July) to a poetic technique (August) and a prose technique (Sept.). The exceptions are the large words which appeared once on every page, about 3/4 of the way through, as I was writing down the seen forehead phrases. Words for Spoke were not seen on any furniture, in the air, or otherwise. This, as far as I can remember, was also pretty much the same technique for the long poems Nijole's House (Potes & Poets Press) and Sixteen (Awede).

Before seeing words I always completed my sentence. The works written prior to August 1972 are: (1) Journals describing early aspects of the clairvoyance as seeing images and energy fields (The Fast, forthcoming from Prospect Books) and a 1971 unpublished journal describing images seen in a summer in Woodstock. (2) The Code Poems (Open Book). These poems and performance pieces from the late 60's used a language found complete in The International Code of Signals. This is a book of ship signals that has been published for mariners since the 18th century, and continually revised. I used both the short incomplete phrases that I found (frequently ending with _____ blank) and complete sentences and questions. (3) Going back further, Magritte Poems, written in the middle 60's and published by Poetry Newsletter in 1970 is a very small pamphlet of 8 non-seen poems describing Magritte paintings in a normal poetic form.

A Short Interlude to Discuss Voices

I did, in the Magritte Poems, use a response to the verse, printed at the back of the poems, giving it a second "voice." In The Code Poems almost all (and I think all the ones published) were a statement and answer between 2 voices, people or ships. Two or three people read the poems aloud in performance. Sometimes I read both parts myself as in the movie "Any Chance of War" and in a non-performance reading situation. The idea of 2 "voices" is natural to The Code Poems as the code was developed for communication between vessels or between mariners lost at sea and a ship.

So the idea of using more than one "voice" or separate "voices" pre-dates the Clairvoyant Journal 1974. To clear up the matter of the three voices in this book, printed in regular type, CAPITALS or italics: at that time—Jan.-June 74—I saw words in a wide variety of sizes, script and printed, on my own forehead (the large capital words on my forehead began in a retreat in June 1973 (Unpublished Journals, 1973)) and on other people, forehead included, and on every other imaginable surface or non-surface; the wall, the typewriter, the paper I was typing on, people's clothes, the air, and even words strung out in the air from the light pull (a favorite place), anywhere.

I bought a new electric typewriter in January 74 and said quite clearly, perhaps aloud, to the words (I talked to them as if they were separate from me, as indeed the part of my mind they come from is not known to me) I have this new typewriter and can only type lower case, capitals or underlines (somehow I forgot, ignored or couldn't cope with in the speed I was seeing things, a fourth voice, underlined capitals) so you will have to settle yourself into three different prints. Thereafter I typed the large printed words I saw in CAPITALS, the words that appeared on the typewriter or the paper I was typing on in <u>underlines</u> (italics) and wrote the part of the journal that was unseen, my own words, in regular upper and lower case.

It turned out that the regular upper and lower case words described what I was doing, the CAPITALS gave me orders, and the <u>underlines</u> or italics made comments. This is not 100% true, but mostly so.

The description of the voices is an integral part of the sentence discussion, as with three or even 2 operating there was scarcely chance to complete the phrase or sentence.

The situation of the voices, and the interruption and overlay, is quite clear if you hear the tape made by New Wilderness Audiographics wherein Sharon Mattlin is a wonderful CAPITALS and bosses me around endlessly. Peggy De Coursey read the italics for March and Regina Beck for April. Unprinted is a tape with Rochelle Kraut reading italics for May and myself alone reading the June Retreat. Peggy and Regina both sound as if they were scolding me. We worked it so that the voices came fast after each other, occasionally speaking in unison and overlapping, and occasionally one of us would an ad-lib comment.

I want to add it was an enormous amount of fun, though hard work requiring a lot of rehearsals to prepare for the tape. Performances were a little freer, requiring less perfection. These readers and others put up with endless work and no or little monetary reward. Sharon used to get a bowl of cereal but she sounded funny in rehearsal and Peggy got fare to Brooklyn.

Since then all my books are written for one voice, though dis-continued and interrupted, and I have the lonesome pleasure of reading them all by myself.

Destruction of the Sentence

From <u>Spoke</u>, July 23:

why did I the me destroy the sentence blurp   because the

rhyme the mind responds thinks quicker THAN WE SPEAK

and answers below the line itself on the page OR WE SEE IT

THE WORDS

In response to Diane Ward's query, summer 84, "Tell me what you think about sentences" I wrote in letters the following, plus some:

What I think about sentences comes from my understanding through clairvoyance and telepathy, dating back to the acid days of the late 60's and early 70's.

(1) Telepathically we receive from each other the spoken sentence. In a house where everyone took a lot of LSD twice I heard people's thoughts as if they had been spoken out loud. Both thoughts were silently directed to me. One woman thought, almost a shout, "get out of my kitchen" and one man said something about helping me with a house if I bought it, and verified the thought out loud, asking me if I'd heard his thought. I heard their natural speaking voices. Differently, Mitch Highfill told me he once heard a whole conversation on LSD that he heard in reality later the next morning. I have never heard a "written" line from someone—or anything they are reading or studying. I never heard any poetry lines I could steal! Only answers to thoughts. Once I saw two people have a silent conversation which they confirmed.

(2) The sentence is always interrupted. Mind 1 that speaks out loud, or writes, is interrupted by mind 2 that is simultaneously preparing the next sentence or answering a question. Therefore the correct form to represent both minds or the complete mind, is an interrupted form. It takes two or three seconds for the thought to form into a sentence, meanwhile another one is being spoken-written. On acid some hippies could hold conversations with two people at once.

From <u>Spoke</u>, July 29:

some complete the interruptions sentence and I careful

don't BECAUSE IT IS ALREADY _{mother} psychic intuition

helps children KNOWN

(3) The interruptions may be hereditary. My mother could go on with an interrupted story after several minutes without going back and repeating a word. The structure of the mind we each have determines somewhat our style of writing and some style therefore as well as . some formation of brain cells may be an inherited quality. I base this partly on findings from an article in <u>Scientific American</u>, The Brain issue, Sept. 79, about brain diseases.

(4) The sentence is unfinished because the mind of the reader or listener supplies the answer (the end) either through telepathically reading the other's mind, or through common knowledge. Or perhaps the reader involves himself with his own ending, which is equally valid.

Sentence Notes and Quotes

Many things happen at once, peculiar to a journal form, to force interruptions. My writing above and below the line incorporates some of this simultaneity. Linear writing must leave out many simultaneous thoughts and events. I am trying to show the mind.

The <u>Clairvoyant Journal</u> shows the mind working in relation to events happening. It was written at any and many times during the day and night whenever I saw the words until it was time to GO TO BE (bed).

<u>Spoke</u> shows the mind in relation to remembered events of the day—what is in the writer's mind as one writes. I wrote it late at night in bed.

From the <u>Clairvoyant Journal</u>, added in very large letters while I was correcting proofs:

STOP TH SENTENC

with the es omitted from <u>the</u> and from the end of <u>sentence</u>—April 17—two of many incomplete words in my books.

From <u>Little Books / Indians</u>, one of several references to the sentence, this one a pun on the jail sentence. "LITTLE BOOK 128 / NEW PAGES I JUST REMEMBER IT":

> Dear Russell
> better in jail
> for a year
> 　　　NOV 15
> than
> DONT FINISH IT
> S E N T E N C E

Comments from <u>Spoke</u> are many.

June 20 "and all continue sentence please"

June 21 "we don't finish this sentence"—last line for that day meaning we don't finish the subject

July 9 "its because I complete the sentence that I make no complete sense sometimes"

July 29 "dont insist on the sentence formation thats all but keep the meaning until thismonth clear"

Aug. 3 "sentence ending is the complete / some ending is the complete ending"

Aug. 3 "its a long paragraph / piece"—the word paragraph can mean a page and sentence can mean a paragraph

Aug. 3 "I musnt concentrate switch CONTEXT the sentence around so Ism / able with it to include p/o/e/t/r/y and some line breaks with the / uneven first as childish / only"

Aug. 14 "so it is concluded also that I am running out of sentences"

Aug. 15 "I was some comfort to the sentence way out west boy laughs"

Aug. 15 "I CANT WRITE ANYTHING ELSE / EXCEPT SENTENCES"

Aug. 15 "on this third week of my jail / sentence"

Aug. 17 "I was j/a/i/l sentence"

Aug. 17 "I was also sentence / conscious"

Aug. 21 "some / FINISH. / sentence. interrupted. by some / STRUCTURE"

Sept. 4 "why complete the sentence anyway question / because seeing with words before I was writing it in"

The Dimishment of the Ego and the Authority of the Author

Begins in The Code Poems with the verse of alternate forms, "He, she, it or _____ can be," which also has to do with de-sexualizing. RAT CAN(ABLE TO)

About the Clairvoyant Journal Ron Silliman says in Poetry Flash, "The very function of clairvoyance in the work of Hannah Weiner is an assault on the homogeneity, the continuity of the ego."

Especially in the Clairvoyant Journal the person writing is bossed around by voices, and gives up her autonomy to the other parts of herself. A relinquishing of constant conscious control to let the other part of the mind dominate. The ego belongs to the conscious part, the writer's voice, and often, or nearly always, I reacted with some ego controlled emotion such as anger or impatience or amusement to the seen words or voices. I gave up my authority to them, indeed the speed at which the words appeared would not allow for a time of complete ego action or thought.

The incomplete and interrupted sentence does away again with the authority of the author, engaging the reader whose own mind will either naturally or by art respond to the delay of the interruptions and the incompleteness. Perhaps the reader, even, is not allowed a consistent or ego building response by the interrupted and incomplete sentence because the writer throws at the reader such a quick multitude of words, phrases, lines and sentences to be put together and finished.

The reader's ego or expectation is further thrown by the occasional running of words together so that rather than put together the reader must pause and separate the words.

Every engagement of the reader breaks down the author's authority over him, and this includes the change of type face size, requiring an adjustment of eye focus and words written above and below the line, giving the reader a field rather than a linear response and increasing his choice. The variety and speed of reader challenges however will keep the reader from building up his own authority as she reads—responds. The author isn't the only one with an ego.

The author's ego is further controlled in <u>Spoke</u> by transference, which means the author transfers the mind of someone else to himself or actually pushes it and seems to be a thing.

Aug. 7 "who am I in the / next page"

Aug. 13 "I was written in"

Aug. 13 "I was original copy"

Aug. 13 "I was also any / person"

Aug. 13 "I was / anybody else"

Aug. 13 "I was also anybody social systems work telepathically"

Aug. 17 "I was quilt"

Transference of another person's thoughts, feelings or even body movements is not uncommon to me, especially in the past, with acid or marijuana, and in the present, with American Indians.

Naming Names

Involves the ego of the person named and has to do (not naming names) with de-personalization. The deciding factor in my books is the psychic factor.

In the early journals (unpublished) people were referred to by one or another letter of their first name (often the last letter) to preserve the anonymity and focus less on an individual personality. As the seen words developed, real names re-appeared and in the Clairvoyant Journal people often have both first and last names mentioned.

Little Books / Indians is about people, and names names. I often refer to myself in the third person, calling myself Sis or Hannah, often misspelled (destroy the ego attachment to the name).

In Spoke, written in 1981, myname (one word) often replaces my own name and name often replaces a real person's name. Many names are still, however, mentioned throughout the book.

In reference to healing, i.e. the diagnosis of illness which is or was one of my psychic powers, naming the individual is obviously essential. Even in this case, however, in Spoke, I sometimes destroyed the real name as in "very paralysed left arm on the name's left hand side" and "west coast name's chest back pains   intro healer" (Aug. 3). This is probably giving into writing's political pressure to de-personalize or perhaps just admitting to myself that people don't like healing diagnosis, especially free from a psychic. Unfortunately these unnamed people cannot use the information to protect themselves medically. Native Americans do not have the same hang-up, considering healing a respected quality.

Some Quotes about the Psychic Predicament

July 9 "Hannah I think terrified the Indians have the most knowledge"

July 9 "I haven't got the nerve to tell everybody the truth"

July 28 "I SOMETIMES WONDER IF writing IT IS period TRUE PERIOD AUGUST because of the many predictions"

There is often a psychic insistence on clarity. From <u>Spoke</u>:

July 29 "I want my meaning clear"

      Pronouns

De-sexualizing the pronouns began in the 60's with <u>The Code Poems</u> line "he, she, it or blank ____" and continued in the <u>Clairvoyant Journal</u> with reference to the words and myself as it. In <u>Little Books / Indians</u> and <u>Spoke</u> there is no play with the pronoun but neither do I ever use the masculine as the indefinite pronoun.

      Closing

I think (opinion) one of the important things about <u>Spoke</u> is said on Aug 14:

      SHOW THE MIND

sis Im writing about included august my mind thinking and SOME
                                   MORE
                            ...MY MIND IS
drunk and has several passages

My mind has also made the decision to call a full length book a novel. This is mentioned in the <u>Clairvoyant Journal</u> and several times in <u>Spoke</u> as follows:

July 28 "sis its all about writing a great big writing novel"

July 28 "sis its a funny book if you like writing a novel"

Aug. 3 "sis its a very long novel book"

Aug. 7 "I have doubtful written this / ...novel"

Aug. 14 "unfinished novel of the type which it in style language and some periods"

Aug. 15 "I am rewriting the prose style"

Aug. 15 "I mean only clairvoyant / material for THE NEXT FOUR YEARS AND THENS I

QUIT / WRITING f / o / r / e / v / e / r which I don't believe"

Aug. 15 "untils I die with only four books / this is included and count journal clair one and this is / it to me...only four books / to be included on the list of the same style per iod"

On Periods

Spoke

Aug. 21 "some periods I must give a lecture / on this subject are"

This book is bound
and publishsed it has a
finished form. It is a closed
book. Also unfinished article.
Open it and write on a
blank page. There are 32
All white   Cross out the
past tense   Say see not saw
Some problem with margins
that come at the end of a line
encouraging long sentences
without cut-offs or discipline
self-indulgent and finished
going on from side to side
even from left
to right because this is
English   It is a closed
form from side to side
The bottom of the page
is coming but so is the next

The next. Endless space
with no lines   Top to
bottom is not important
until the end. Then it will
end. Bound. Cannot tear
out a sheet or add one or
get another book. Not
notebook. Not for notes.
For another sentence
Some have periods   Some
Not to tease the mind
Not to blip the alpha wave
Not to challenge the language
Just get from side to side
Get to another bottom
Realize limits
                    ON THIS PAGE

On this page I describe
white   Vanilla ice cream
without a chocolate chip
in sight   Oval and
shining with a black strap
bathing cap   The page
quality paper with
texture slightly off
Cotton sheets with pillow
cases   You don't say
matching unless it's a color
or a print   PRINT JUST A
LITTLE   Rolled about three
inches long and stuffed
or flat and crisp   cigarette
paper   It used to be
chocolate or banana and long
It used to be every sponse
had a response   Now it
dont   we are accustomed
The white race is late.

The white race is late coming
to consciousness said Coyote
It didn't live with wild
animals or many-colored
birds   It always
wore clothes   The white
race is on this page
written in ink of color
The white race uses a lot
of periods. and some...
a lot of the white race
goes to church and here
in this country many are
white   Many have steeples
All have doors   The winter
is white here too   So are
the paintings of Robert
Ryman   and the frames
on many other pictures
hanging on white walls
The walls of the Whitney
are white   Here is the end

Here is the end which is at
the beginning

the beginning of this page
Here is the end which is at
you ever think of that
when you write it did
when you read it only
The pause is not noticeable
and causes a pause
space is decreasing now
on another line the white
or legible room for legible
another will it be clear
and one line runs into
the top of the page comes
not enough space when
different   what if there's
your way up it's not so
at the bottom and work
backwards so you start
This page is going to be written

This page is going to be written
forward   All the words and
lines follow one another
in sequence   Like the world
was created and Adam was
made if you read the book
which tells that story
Otherwise forward begins
in the sea flaps to the
shore and grows legs
stands up and beats its wife
Then we have history
and culture and social
science and institutions
Institutions is a long
word with three i's
I's denote ego the self
which is already defined
with only one i but 2 e's
making thee or he <u>and</u> she
and pronouns make more
people all with ego's and i's
all i's are on this page

All eyes are on this page
including a change of spelling
to coincide with the change

of meaning   That's not very
clever but is how the
language spells itself
including some meanings
Meanings make you think
of about instead of what's
on the page   about is a
word you can use all by
itself which is a pronoun
referring   Referring is a
long article about the
referrent which attaches
reminds and is owned
Itself is owned by about
They lock you up for such
nonsense

WHICH

which is a play on words
by witches of writing
We know all the meanings
and all the property which
caused a scandal for several
centuries   But you can't
own the mother earth
This is a sacred tradition
preserving the gold under
ground where no one can
be greedy about it and
keeping the uranium buried
so no one can blow
allthemselves up   There are
politics everywhere including
the language which commands
obedience to its meaning
Be careful what you say
in a business letter because
people conform   All the
treaties were broken so
written is not the truth

Written is not the truth
How many lies can you
find on this page? I am
35 years old and writing
my first poem.   Three
periods have been used
so far   Jackson will be

pleased because this is
just writing   Bruce will
die from the sequence and
Abigail will cut up all
her film again   Abigail
and Henry are people
Charles is a writer with no
two words alike   Barbara
who gave me this book
takes pictures and put
none in this book leaving
me room for description
of people and words which
are written
                    BLANK PA

BLANK PA

                              GE

ge a shortened form of gee
or get or gentlemen or gerund
but none of these are useful
                    G
is spelling a letter
which stands for gum

bubble and chew and is
printed or type
in the middle of the line
The middle of the line is
equi-distant between the
margins and is something
I do in my books   Look
to right or left when reading
this G or crossing the street
Useful information is not
always dull   Neither is
shiny   The bottom of
the dull whi^te page with
margins is coming up
soon - coming up as
soon as I get this
writing down to it

Writing down to it now
from the very top with all
this white space to please
White are hills with snow
where I skied on black
skis with white letters
when I was owned by a
business firm in the culture
I put lace and flowers
and buttons on things to please
White sold the best
Sheep are nautral white
which is unbleached and
undyed when you make
coats blankets and
sweaters   We weave and
possess to keep warm
we cut and stitch and
package and ship and sell
all across the world to
keep warm   Some industry
is necessary   Likely none
of it will go
              WHITE SHEEP

White sheep come in black
and grey and brown
giving us a natural variety
in sentences   All the

sentences here are completed
just as sheep have feet
and walk on them   Complete
is useful to a sheep but
not to a sentence which can
stop anywhere and let
you fill in the
If you read minds or
poetry you can do this
Something else is unfin
          I LIKE BLAN

LIKE BLAN and I add a K
for kitchen which is useful
and white sometimes especially
if you're poor   If you're
poor you have a white sink
but you might have a
stainless steel one if you
are rich or a restaurant
The woman said
she was white as cheese which
goes in the refrigerator which
is likely to be white but
you can paint it   White
foods that go in the refrigerator
are cheese sour cream cream
milk fish and Cool Whip
Foods that are white inside
are onions potatoes and
apples   The Indians have
a joke about apples that
means you might work
for the government   You
can guess what the joke is

The joke is because of
financial difficulties, the
Leonard Peltier Defense Committee
can no longer offer Crazy
Horse Spirit free to all
people on the mailing list
which is irony   Or perhaps
not   In order to receive the   .
next copy please send this
subscription blank and
your payment ($10 a year,

Low Income $5 a year) to the
Leonard Peltier Defense Committee
2524 16th Ave So., Seattle,
Wash. 98144   Even if you
absolutely cannot pay any-
thing which is how an
Indian newspaper addresses
its readers asking for an
immediate stop to the
brutal conditions at Marion

brutal conditions at Marion
Penitentiary, an immediate
transfer for Leonard Peltier
and so (seen) with the spirit
of Crazy Horse we close.

Tempting myself pen in hand the writer
to equi-distance between margins I turn
the book awkwardly and write the long way
the long way across the page with the cover
flopping over and no even surface
to write on

THIS IS PRINCIPLE

This is principle to sacrifice comfort
for a long line equi-distant between
margins and sleep on the floor between walls
Between walls is where all the furniture is
and the books and the people

THAT IS SPACE

That is space longer across than down
that I write on and contrary to habit
The white space stilll goes from left to right
and we read the words across and then
down

THIS IS SLEEP

This is sleep we could write this in
or read this in the sleep of consciousness
which imposes no telling the truth (seen)
is just telling a little tale alertness
to grasp meaning or language

THIS IS LANGUAGE

This is language this is written in but
the ordinary form of the simple spoken
word

THIS IS OMITTED

This is omitted - thedifficulty and
pleasure of language used to open
and tempt the mind of the reader
to new experience and new form

THIS IS OBJECTIVE

This is objective although this is also
my personal experience as a writer
and the personal experience of writing
goes down with each word on the page

THIS IS WORD

This is word spelled backwards is drow
which is how English amuses me
because you can draw in the a

THIS IS IMPOSSIBLE

This is impossible to finish at one
sitting

AND SO

SO WE CONTINUED

continued
seen (necessary
line breaks) vary
across the slant of
the page each line
a different space to the margin
confusing the breath of the mind
the length of the thought on the
page is flat and has an edge
and to disobey the government of the
margin is to lose theline out to

like out to the edge me or
swimming in a short pool
I feel a few more strokes of the
pen are necessary to complete me
forming words which will
sometime be read and space
and less space which
inhibits the hand
and fewer words
come from
the

the
pen or the
mind of the
reader or writer
whoever interprets
this simple sentence
will have written it
the owner of the line is the
margin which refuses to give
any sense of rhythm in this
varied length the expectation is
confused in the mind and the hand
and each beginning of a line must be
begun anew with a different rhythm
or expectation or whatever word will fit
in the space left out to the margin
This is writing slantwise diagonally
across the page and gives no
consolation either of sound
or of word groups it
just finishes the
space and
repeats
itself

itself
writes about
itself writing
on a slant across
the page and does
not put in the word
that was thought of for
lack of space   the line
thought of running was lost
but was about form and space

form and space make it difficult
to say everything but so does history
and political aesthetics allow leaflet
but not leaf   not even the leaf of
a book that's a page   the question
is whether the margin should stand
and is the end of the page a natural
law perhaps the best thing
is to   FINISH THE PAGE
and let the reader decide

some disobedience
here

here
a blank
book complete-
ly engaging
the reader to be
writer and so be-
coming a book written
by the writer which it
was not to begin with
it was not to begin with a book
with words or pictures in it and so said
how much blankness will engage
the reader to become writer and now
the blankness is going away and
the white space is filled by this pen
and the margins have not given in
but have varied themselves
and so has the space this
is because a book was
not written this book
is written and
soon comes
to an end
that

that
repeat word
comes soon
on a new page
and the whiteness
is gone and the
margins met on four
sides of the page and

agreed to keep the writing
inside   This is the law of
the margin even when broken the
what is lost is the word is lost but
can be repeated on another line
giving in to a form of concensus
a meeting an agreement of four
and the agreement about finishing comes
with the last page which is next and
after that there is no more that
finishes an attempt to fill
in all the spaces left
by a writer in a
published
completely
blank
book

book
is what it
is called and
this is the last
page still slanti
out to the margin
and still written with pen
and a phrase at the bottom
appears just to vary the style
not too much concerned with
ending but filling out to the margin
spaces until the end of the page some
where along the space diminishes
and the last page finishes the book
something could be said about the
number of pages of which the
division is sixteen and ten
and six and something
could be said about
finishing the page
when there is
no more
space
left
AND THIS PAGE

There are other ways to write 0I234
Federal Prison Hospital Sprin Misso
We're open for discussion this0 after
Failing to win any assur from0
the Guatemalan regime that0 it0I2
Here's some sentence mater 0I234
Leonard Gwarth - ee - lass Pelti AIM0I
That's very interesting. The coast guard
would refrain from any such0 attac
Write me and we'll keep in0I2 conta
Greetings Brothers & Sisters frien and0I
You try to get close to natur 0I234
Mexican interior secretary name0 inclu
There is no reason for this sente to0I2
understand with the same feeli and0I
love I have for not only all0I thing
in life but for you also0 0I234
I would like very much to0I2 read0
dismantling of the 89 official refug camps
Here we meet again. Ah but0I I0I23
one third of the population is0I2 now0I
on a hunger strike 0I234 0I234
Take this sentence out! 0I234 0I234
sheltering 46,000 Guatemalans in0I2 the0I
I reminded you of its exist 0I234
This will keep us safe from0 viole
To hear the broadcast in your0 commu
refugees are being given the0I optio
an art of balance, purity and0I seren
Today my brothers and I begin our0I
journey to oo ope wakan kin retur to0I2
the bosom of the creator 0I234 0I234
postcards have wonderful simpl sente
returning to Guatemala or reset in0I2
I.49 can you imagine that0 0I234
Today we take the sacred road0 and0I
begin our fast for life 0I234 0I234
a stated opinion, esp one given after
the Valle of Edznor in Campe state
I know a couple of old Yanke fello
liked the location very much0 0I234
Two guards were murdered in0I2 separ
There Are Seven Words In This0 Sente
I25 miles north of the Chiapas borde regio
deliberation; a decision; deter 0I234
incidents in the infamous contr unit0
I think she understands by0I2 now0I

new settlements in the border area0 would
The first sentence was very diffi to0I2
This prison is one of the most0 moder
I retired last August 0I234 0I234
60?000 refugees in Chiapas outsi the0I
The next sentence should becom easie
on June 26, I975 two FBI agent part0
of a 40 man paramilitary force on0I2
Pine Ridge, opened fire on0I2 a 0I23
turtles, made in the form of0I2 the0I
island were the first official coins of 0I2
In Guatemala I954 marks the0I viole
Such sentences are sometimes calle full0
Standing Deer, Leonard Pelti and0I
Rechaza will continue to a death fast0
due to the abridgement of their relig
I remain silent most of the0I time0
in I954, the CIA with the suppo of0I2
hot hot hot here today took0 famil
prisoners are beaten at random mistr and0I
developing commercial trans resul
in the creation of money 0I234 0I234
the I954 counterrevolution opene the 0I
way for the military to firml estab
distinguished from minor sente which
The most serious report I0I23 have0
ever been written up for is0I2 escap
Keep your spirits up 0I234 0I234
Aided by CIA pilots and0I fight
This Sentence May Be Divid And0I
Re-United Into Ten Words 0I234 0I234
Will I never be allowed to pray0 in0I2
smashing 60th birthday join0 us0I2
International workers' solidarity day0I was0I

Brotherhood, Unity, Solid Support
I am most inter in0I2 having some news about the0I poets
a youngster from0 mexic and a youngster from the Domin Repub
they burn cedar 0I234
This sentence feels so0I2 light...
when we cannot pract our0I religion as has been practiced
by0I2 our0I ancestral parents
In Guatemala in0I2 the0I highlands there are hundreds and0I
hundr of Indian villages
there's a histo resto
but after all a0I23 littl simplicity a little since 0I234
when we have no0I2 recou to justice in greeds iron house 0I234
there are pow wows0 and0I more pow wows; it is the0I pow0I
wow season in Oklahoma! 0I234 0I234
whole sentences erupt up0I2 and fall
traditional place some0 of them thousands of years old0I 0I234
so you want to0I2 be0I2 a triathlete? Here's how
THEN IT IS TIME TO0I2 RETUR TO THE CREATOR
The factory where I0I23 worke was located in the Rue Temple 0I234
0I234
how effective it0I2 will0 be I dont know
There the Mayans have0 lived poorly, respectfully, and most of0I2
the0I time, peacefully
Do not understand this0 stene
The Prisoners defen commi signed
he was found lying face0 down on a rock
Ask them to order the0I abolishment of the Control Unit 0I234 0I234
The past four years have0 been a nightmare
can't believe this0 is0I2 happening is written
I like to be those peopl who are bilingual
This is the first time0 this sentence is being used and0I some0
sentences should not have0 sauce (sources?)
WHAT YOU CAN DO0I2 0I234
I learned how to0I2 dance since I was small
An already repre gover went insane
Theories dont make0 a0I23 good picture
Leonard Peltier suppo group PO Box 326
strike ball just0 misse
what it says is0I2 separ and the way it says it disco 0I234
in the Western Hemis they0 started to kill Indians 0I234 0I234
If they can steal our0I land and put me in jail then0 they0
can steal your land and put you0I in0I2 jail
What d'ya say ya0I2 wanna roll out of here. Yeah.
What is Connected to0I2 this0 Sentence
Between I5 and 30,000 have0 been killed
I have all of these books that I read and I read legen and0I I read
stories

Cutting our wrist or0I2 hanging ourselves would mean0 there were
just three more dead india who0I were victimized into suicide 0I234
0I234
a word full of0I2 the0I letter c
whole villages some0 5000I or more people
The old fourtheenth amend equal protection by law
It is not a suici nor0I a hunger strike we seek it0I2 is0I2 a
DEATH FAST
I am working for0I pay0I at the Native American cente here0 in
Oklahoma City
the belief that you0I can0I say what you want or lie about it0I2
massacred by machi gun0I, by machete
How far do they0 go0I2? As far as the car.
Thanks to these dista colon humble Greek villages became opule citie
Infamous Mario Illin Penitentiary Death Fast
grenades tossed into0 packe churches, packed schoolrooms 0I234 0I234
one could go on
He can learn about every culture
One or more THES0 have0 been used in one or sente 0I234

```
Civil disob at the CIA and the Defense
240I2 goes0 right over the bridge into
TheOI only0 real in writing is writing itself
India relig services have been temporarily suspended
Socia worke for Peace and Nuclear Disarm
Youre pitch toward home plate
Which is0I2 coincidental with a slow
braki a0I23 release, a bombardment, a
TVs0I will0 be installed in our cell block
I0I23 make0 him a very intellectual cultural
cat0I he0I2 really speaks two languages
June0 9th0I March from Dag Hammerskjold
Words in0I2 configurations fresh to our senses
Relig servi will be viewed by videotape
Read0 Jacks Mac Low's note on the back
On0I2 behal of the "disappeared" people in
Guate since I965, 35,000 persons have
TheOI formi of a question, for exit takes
place aroun and about this sway.
Aim0I direc in Prison 89637-I32
All0I of0I2 those islands they say is so
TheOI refug desire to remain in Chiapas
Still a0I23 smart person without rhyme
Becau of0I2 mode of confinement of prisoners
You0I want0 to discuss the prohibition
Recen event in a camp called "Las Delicias"
Devoi of0I2 troubling or obsessive subject
News0 media is no longer allowed inside this
Id0I2 like0 to go to China.  Yeah
After theOI attack on El Chupadero
Why0I not0I just write??  Try it again!
Youll like0 it
TheOI illeg covert drug research programs
TheOI goal0 of this class is to acquire
Frenc conve skills
3I000 Resid of that camp fled to Las Delicias
locat furth away from the border
Pleas recyc this catalogue
all0I cell0 furniture, table, chair, shelves
and0I cloth pegs, mirror to shave have
been0 perma removed from the cells
Quest are0I split over blackness themselves
Reloc theOI refugees as far as Campeche
Makin pleas that which should be removed
Priso shoes were confiscated and never
How0I am0I2 I going to.  Impossible
Offer churc owned farmland for resettling
```

TheOI survi of the priarie dog is proof
posit that0 both Hegel and Kant were wrong
in0I2 their understanding of the "New World"
My0I2 peopl thank you for your help
Al10I of0I2 the nouns write
The0I gover began relocation to Campeche
Howev I0I23 stay home and save money
Leona Pelti was one of some forty young
India who0I came to the defense of the
Sis0I there has to be a stop to your sentences
Six0I hundr of the 3,100 refugees at Las Delicias
My0I2 famou accent. How I would love to get rid
No0I2 one0I knows who shot the agents
I0I23 the0I last sentence is perhaps the most
25000 fled0 and are now occupying Diocese
And0I of0I2 course name mentioned on the VL
The0I reser was swarming with Swat teams
Ive0I notic repetition
About 46000 refugees live in UN financed
I0I23 was0I expected to be there by eight in
My0I2 impri is your imprisonment
When0 I0I23 was fifteen I knew an old
lady0 she0I was clairvoyant
Here0 lies0 the next to the last sentence
Large refug camps Monday killing six of
It0I2 is0I2 patently clear that many of
the0I state that have been released
by0I2 the0I FBI regarding the incident
I0I23 can0I write nice stories about my cat
Youd0 have0 to be a little unstable to give
There is0I2 no Mexican military detachment
We0I2 strug for the freedom of all the
peopl and0I for our sacred earth

```
Norma I0I23 would compl about it0I2 0I234
She0I promi us0I2 life0 only0 as0I2 long0
as0I2 the0I pipe0 and0I cerem were0 kept0
A0I23 compl word0 a0I23 phras an0I2 inter
Mexic army0 tortu and0I kille three Guate
A0I23 lovin tribu to0I2 a0I23 spect organ
A0I23 lifel tenan advoc and0I a0I23 wonde
The0I admin at0I2 Mario is0I2 in0I2 viola
of0I2 the0I const of0I2 the0I Unite State
and0I the0I great laws0 of0I2 the0I creat
The0I econo was0I immed trans 0I234 0I234
Refug last0 week0 and0I has0I denie food0
Runni and0I bikin are0I fairl easy0 thing
Ask0I them0 to0I2 end0I priso oppre in0I2
The0I name0 of0I2 the0I const 0I234 0I234
Go0I2 beyon form0 to0I2 achie poetr 0I234
Thous of0I2 refug along the0I Mexic Guate
He0I2 got0I off0I the0I plane jump0 on0I2
Yet0I it0I2 canno get0I ACA0I accre 0I234
Thoug dicta all0I exerc of0I2 reaso and0I
The0I trans of0I2 refug from0 the0I jungl
Hanna I0I23 have0 a0I23 wonde time0 0I234
Strip of0I2 our0I perso prope and0I legal
Every esthe or0I2 moral preoc being absen
A0I23 spoke for0I the0I unite natio high0
You0I could eithe do0I2 it0I2 or0I2 you0I
The0I sweet aroma of0I2 sweet and0I Cedar
It0I2 is0I2 diffi for0I me0I2 to0I2 speak
Inves the0I situa in0I2 the0I camps at0I2
Swimm is0I2 somet that0 takes a0I23 lot0I
Each0 morni and0I eveni with0 their praye
My0I2 paint is0I2 born0 in0I2 a0I23 state
Mexic decid in0I2 late0 April to0I2 move0
Oh0I2 thats going to0I2 be0I2 highl quest
incid are0I eithe false unsub or0I2 clear
Greek sailo gave0 the0I Phoen stiff compe
46000 Guate refug from0 camps along the0I
It0I2 is0I2 nice0 to0I2 recei a0I23 lette
The0I strug is0I2 not0I simpl a0I23 strug
Hallu provo by0I2 some0 shock or0I2 other
To0I2 a0I23 centr locat in0I2 the0I state
They0 have0 to0I2 go0I2 into0 these feder
Stand Deer0 and0I Recha are0I my0I2 broth
Nowad I0I23 rarel start a0I23 pictu from0
Campe I250I miles north of0I2 the0I borde
I0I23 was0I in0I2 the0I plane on0I2 the0I
I9730 I9750 2000I India kille in0I2 viole
```

```
Objec or0I2 subje I0I23 am0I2 entir irres
A0I23 moder army0 suppl by0I2 the0I Unite
State and0I Israe blaze a0I23 trail of0I2
Did0I you0I do0I2 a0I23 lot0I in0I2 your0
Myrtl Poor0 Bear0 signe a0I23 third affid
Stres the0I reali of0I2 the0I word0 0I234
Gunme repor dress in0I2 Guate Army0 unifo
What0 you0I see0I is0I2 what0 you0I get0I
I9760 Leona Pelti was0I arres in0I2 Canad
That0 I0I23 am0I2 runni out0I of0I2 sente
Trail of0I2 scorc earth massa and0I decim
You0I could have0 taken two0I aspir 0I234
We0I2 share the0I spiri of0I2 the0I creat
Poetr funct is0I2 to0I2 rekin langu to0I2
Parti of0I2 the0I left0 was0I rende impos
I0I23 have0 a0I23 frien named Joe0I I0I23
The0I cry0I of0I2 priso activ priso refor
Offic verse cultu is0I2 more0 a0I23 celeb
Inten death squad attac and0I kidna of0I2
You0I can0I quote me0I2 I0I23 dont0 want0
Trans to0I2 anoth priso where we0I2 can0I
The0I twent or0I2 as0I2 later from0 colla
Bodie were0 aband on0I2 July0 60I23 on0I2
Then0 I0I23 would just0 write a0I23 norma
In0I2 your0 lette be0I2 sure0 you0I menti
Break it0I2 langu away0 from0 its0I enfor
The0I mass0 based labor and0I peasa organ
So0I2 we0I2 went0 to0I2 the0I cafe0 in0I2
Hospi facil consi of0I2 a0I23 bare0 steel
THE0I enlar sente howev allow as0I2 a0I23
Mexic soldi total destr all0I food0 suppl
He0I2 was0I watch TV0I2 he0I2 got0I a0I23
Stand Deer0 Recha and0I mysel have0 been0
Beate witho provo Stand Deer0 is0I2 620I2
One0I or0I2 more0 THEs0 have0 been0 used0
Force under while last0 month the0I entir
```

The words in capitals are seen

This is a dreadful sentence from So

If granted by Congress at the levels requested

The edge I mean is on the right

She made language in her own eager style

Has the D.A. given in

Have I started to move from the left

A lot of the things are lyrics

words move from left to right

At Big Mountain they are moving the Navajos

A provocative personal notice

A real margin is on both left and right

My Madagascar Imperial is a stamp

The left hand edge is often even

The stamp where is the stamp

THE PROSPECT

stamps^{can come from a window}

The left hand edge for most people is the same

   or similar

Even I even it out by starting at the left

The Shining Path is in Peru

How can you actually proceed from socialism toward

   communism?

Every word brings me closer to the edge

Something like nouns are a comfort

Illusions of change

The development of a skilled and intelligent

   foreign policy

The assassination of the union's Secretary moves across

   the page like any other sentence

The disappearance and assassination of four other union

   activists goes all the way to the right hand margin

   and back again twice

They have adopted original forms of protest

   is fairly short

We united the left hand margin and the right hand margin

   with words

We all of us do it   WE DO IT

Scores of Guatemalans who disappeared during the
    last two years are at the bottom of rivers
    is only part of a sentence
The longer sentences go back and forth between
    the margins
According to Garcia many had lost their minds
They may have been killed or transferred to other
    jails
He tried to hang himself twice but the rope was too
    thin starts on the left
Whatever we say starts at the left even if it is
    about atrocities
All sentences share the same fate moving from left
    to right
The Guatemalan disappeared account for 30%
We mobilize national and international public opinion

This is the first time I've written this sentence

That is not my own sentence

Whosever it is, it ends on the right

Politics should move in the opposite direction of
    the sentence

Also known as issue oriented artists

Political art is coming on strong

The sub-committee recommended against the restoration
    of so-called lethal military

Yet another victim of "disappearance" last month was
    Brother

It is not always necessary to finish the sentence

Comprising the Guatemalan National Revolutionary
    Unity (URNG)

Or even to begin it

The second rights activist to die has neither beginning
    nor end

The sentence structure goes on forever

THE SENTENCE PERIOD

Beginning at the left at the top of the page

The constant reiteration of form

The ending at the right hand edge

The disappearance of many people

The movement to the bottom of the page

Covering blank space line by line

Constitution by military decree

October's scheduled presidential election

A new tax on non-quota coffee exports

Victims of political violence in Guatemala

Deaths are first to be suffered by rights group

Rights is not right

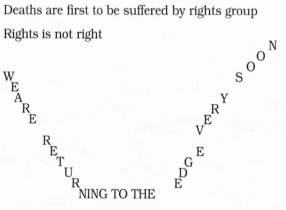

Had notion to teach Ed said no write for newsletter went swimming all ideas went away but here they are back personal style writing and paragraph.

If you are a poet would you have the three obligations, work on yourself to become more conscious, work in the world to change it free and equal include ecological survival, and work in poetic forms that themselves alter consciousness.

As for work on the self many poets write to understand themselves, thus endless subjective "I" a technique that belongs in our time more to the realm of psychoanalysis or meditation. Very few of us can add to anyone else's consciousness by repeating personal history. I speak also the opposite exceptions myself recording clairvoyant experiences and those who live in situations that need clarification before social change can be made. To anyone who insists on writing "I" would she concentrate on another and write that person's being and thought. It would shift to the other, still incorporating understanding problem of self. Are you telepathic   you can do so   the mind can be strong and have power be kind   you can be felt.

Next paragraph the work in the world whether done actually in life by taking political action (and I would everyone would one time or another lend her power to social change it is a dedication consciousness obligates) or whether done in the writing here by exception I accept meaning political change can be accomplished at every level of consciousness and begin another say paragraph.

Work on the poetic form although in my ordinary, non-clairvoyant consciousness I write reader in sentence form believe techniques of disjunctive, non-sequential, non-referential writing can directly alter consciousness, whether by destroying long habits of rationality, by surprise tactics to which the brain responds differently, or by forcing a change to alpha level by engaging both hemispheres of the brain, choose your science. Thus would destroy meaning, as overproduced as capital goods, and concentrate consciousness on the letter, parts of words, word, phrase, or even the non-sequential sentence on the page. Messages come silently anyway to those who learn.

An elevated awareness (if the word consciousness is objectionable) has more power and is more politically effective, more intelligent thus better writing, include personal survival.

Look always for the work to be done. I also spell revolution without an r and poetry without a p. Class dismissed.

25 May, 1989

This is what I said at the church without comments

future Journal clear   It is important to note that my mind gave me directions Clairvoyant Journal not only relating to future events but also relating to what I needed. As I am thinking about how to write about the Indians responding to need an Indian calls from Oklahoma So his mind   knows and is open. The indians know by mind and respond according to need. I suppose this is a way to a cooperative socialist society. You have to be willing to help intelligent included. The only time I have seen white people responding by mind to need was the last time I was in Woodstock where the mind prevailed, 1971. This is something for the future to be had by white people and black also and more give in.

I think there are four ways the poet of the future can work, and you can combine them also. One is to work politically, ecologically, whatever work that needs to be done in the world, one is to raise the level of as I explained consciousness (this I think is done by like us language some other poets of course using disjunctive, non-sequential techniques) one is to work with power, and disguise yourself that quits keep clear about writing new poetry. Meaning grounds you in your every day speaking consciousness and cannot alter the mind by technique. Alter the mind and you work politically with greater effect understanding like also some great readers who use power on us say who twice refused but sometimes he can be felt and includes by without language like us like who refused to help at the church and kept silent. The mind obeys unconsciously giving strict orders that are agreed upon by someone who twice dying explains without giving clear motives like once clairvoyant journal explained. Copy this letter and keep a copy with you when you talk about language until you remember entirely forgiven embarrassment this. sis conclude I also mentioned that you could read the mind two of the poet concluded who sits near you for future like me spell society explained by culture that's like the society culture two Hannah we spoke included by reference thinking again conclude with a poet who knows the next mind is cant you the journal does make it clear to him understand included that you can read the mind of a person sitting or far away forgiven hang up. May, 1989 mother concludes some extra material for the future begin to notice who responds to your thinking and who obeys your silent instructions when you say often sis silent persons instruct alone continue with complete say often that you telephone complete persons who are silent like me twice because you can answer their shut up conclude

Sis explain energy we feel slightly without call it power when we are like Hannah allergy to pillow we read the mind by sitting sis complain the we felt someone until the end of his talk and believed from for his mind like concert. Sis we call it just in our bliss we feel content praised and make it clear that power can enjoy healing sitting close. Some healing included when you reach that clear state beloved and keep closing the opposition someone hurts politically Hannah we close the minds of those who oppose us so they can't feel their power like someone does often say who mention names Allen has tried. We feel the power opposed. Sis like I recorded in an early journal like twice. The Fast didn't explain much but it hurts to be unpublished like others without important make it clear that you were learning and the Clairvoyant Journal said made it clear that we ourselves follow our minds when we do things like reading. Justify control clear Hannah I write this letter to let you know I am understanding always like Indians. Follow your instructions and keep your wife keep clear obedient say always like often happens among two close. This is strict like someone whose name Leonard is often reminded. Clear the pipe. I omit invitation until you understand sacrifice meaning like clear. Sis conclude your letter with a document like Leonard gave pipe. Understand recluse obedient obey signals obedience rules culture subliminally without constriction. Sis pipe obeys document unclear two periods honest invitation when you he returns like quick obey signals on street with those who are Hannah he knows be quick with strict obedience like ourselves friends complete sign

hannah

document recorded in Douglas when obedient make clear said I could forgive live on the South with children and be buried among the Indians if I wished before I kept my mother handle the agreement final with poetry generation follows power and agreement signed by Leonard by will Hannah's period concluded enjoy book when document finished complete and obedient children listen hurry poetry included generation follows in say their silent culture tradition book follows from Mary published which published enjoyed herself when a young girl Indian with grandparents say sold when published abroad German later published I think abroad Entitled to money handle their land differently when included Enjoy smoking pipe Leonard gave me on visit when you and Susan come understanding forgiven argument anyway just be important when you are without any around to clear yourself. Make public document please honest required poetry included future public

NARRATIVE (Abigail Child and Hannah Weiner)

ac   We come
        a daily news full field
        even if inexorably false
        is rearranged
        in order our knowing makes

hw   memory requires agree d
        place takes in time
        instantaneous is knowing
        in lacking surprise sequence
        reason describe involve

ac   until the day arrives
        to interpose a porous scene
        contradict
        in counterpoint surrounds
        our consciousness of time

hw   connection relation explanation
        meaning maintains destroy
        length
        slow a non do it
        speed respond power

ac   propose blank space
        for each in echoes of omission takes
        to articulate an inattention
        I-he-you-her-
        implausible

hw   historical
        switch sink bathroom
        in syntax silently
        change political record
        language consciousness imagealter

ac   promises
            an array of conjugation
            The wish you want
            to criticize is mortality
            rupture

hw   comfort
        causal rational
        hinting more than
        elders only story

ac   revives in passion amps
            arms
            ams
            insubordination

hw   inturrupt nuzhe letter
        authorita bk sentence
        algosaib said
        page continue turn

or related questions of your own choice, bus Halifax to Todmordon I am writing in my ordinary consciousness and use a more normal syntax train Hebden Bridge to Halifax with more meaning   In my other, clairvoyant consciousness bus Queensbury to Bradford I follow my seen words' instructions and attempt to train Bradford to Leeds *destroy meaning, disrupt syntax* and STOP TH SENTENCE bus Queensbury to Bradford   The point is to *show the mind* Meaning grounds one in one's ordinary consciousness bus Leeds to Kirkstall Abbey   Disjunctive, non-sequential, non-referential writing can alter bus Leeds to Branhope consciousness bus Queensbury to Haworth allowing what is the equivalent of my seen words train Haworth to Keighley to enter ordinary consciousness   This other consciousness often knows the future train Keithley to Bradford and knows what is in others' minds   It is much more intelligent bus Bradford to Ilkley than the consciousness of the subject "I" and can be more politically effective   I see my work bus Queensbury to Bradford in a context of other minds   I find most interesting the work of those bus Halifax to Shibden Hall who write as described above, breaking down the authority of syntax and sentence with some exceptions, which is a reversal bus Shibden Hall to Halifax   Linguistically inevitable historically this work as a new way to alter consciousness bus Halifax to Queensbury brings with it some (spiritual) power   This can be used to change the culture bus Bradford to Queensbury (Poets of other persuasions also have power)   There is an old similar argument of mantra versus prayer versus chant versus silence trail Ilkley to Bradford   I like poets who are politically engaged   This is work that can be understood at all levels of consciousness train Bradford to Scarborough here I like meaning   The most disturbing things associated with poetry are that poets are read mostly by each other and that a poet who writes one way often opposes a poet who writes another barge along Rochdale canal   Other poets are the useful sources train Scarborough to Huddersfield   Universities play a role for me only if I am taught in them or if similar poets are train Huddersfield to Leeds are taught (and teach) in them   Yes I believe the system can be changed from within train Leeds to Bradford because power has the ability to open others to power and a strong mind can transfer itself   In ten years I will be seventy years old and will in my life as a poet been bus Bradford to Queensbury a performer, a clairvoyant, a "language" poet and a friend to the traditional Native American movement Worth Valley railway   I would wish that we understand each other silently and that we (poets and) form a concensus and a model for a new culture train Halifax to Manchester   I would wish that only women could vote.

now a preditious matterman is a masterman
ma please
                        now for the historical
marm   im confused   how many generations back
                        well alright   now for the story telling
details   submit for
who ma
                        ulysses s suffragette   you might want to
put that in
marm im hidden
                        mubject atter   we like mubject atter
                        so exciting   so intensification
                        colibacy comes next   ohmigosh
marm please underage
marm please the communest party is a new thing to us   it has
never gone bust
                        very well   the union suit is a green check
50¢
pshaw
ma im disappointed   im really tormented inside   im really
a great big teacher
                            yer better say watcha teachin son
puff puff   well i thought id teach bicycle riding today
please ma please   im really tormented   those little critturs
                        yer mean chipmunks are easy
ma please its my turn
the comminform   marm please maybe she could explain
                        no no i wont
ma please were trying to sneak it in
                        the mrumph cant
marm the you know   the comminform we dont know it
                        dont bother   stalin stupid
please marm i only want a directorship

                              very well   im an anarchist
single marm
ma please not a new vocabulary structure
i might be absent due to a subdeterminate of the
plausible clause

                              well yer better get some food in
predatory animals have moths to eat   what do you have
                              fettuccine the master of the platter
                              well i suppose thats a fancy word for
spaghett
ma please the banana peels   could we sell them   we dont
know what to do with them

                              concessions stand   discount
were trying to get some french cuisine out here
what do you do with those frogs feet after you eat them frogs legs
                              no no you mustnt   thats definitely a
categorical disapprovement
marm where did she get the corn muffin
bakery only two miles
ma she didnt leave
please marm   the corn muffin thats hard marm
                              his wife has to bake them   thats the
problem

                              now to getting the work done
                              aunt han   i am revolutionam   we mustnt
disagree over

                              details   we do not nam   i think you
understand

                              places dates and details are posted daily
womens dispe
marm please the outhouse is the only place we all go
                              well get it into print
an affiliated stanza marm   can i have one
                              very well the temporal dissertation is a
notification   grrrr

                              now my first disappearance performance is

                                    170

on page

        well we have a decided development here

fyrranththrapus

        i would say that was a definitely

implausible communest

        quote
        i was jailed for that

marm the britches at the institute wouldnt accept my paper
it was printed on the left hand column only

        well write without gurdj

who marm

        a teacher   hes the one who made you climb

six stories up the wall
was there a rope marm

        urmph   pour the l

marm please complete the you know
suppose i were blacklisted marm   where would i be   on the front
or the back page

        well the colibacy question   are you sure its

clear
marm no one comes to the meetings   aunt oops   ma shes 104

        credential card   well we always had

several

        well im going out to tea
        well we know what paws gonna dee

smoocheroo marm skiss   mm mmm skiss   kisseroo

        well what happened
        nine months will tell the true

really marm lunchbreak   we sons in la want an afternoon off
marm im hungry i ate the barricade

        were they jellusade

CUSTARD

        marm the communest banns are up   what

are banns

        dont marry   grab and scram
        oh no no no   veritable

word ma

                              definitely grumph   disallowed
multi sexual obligations   what are those marm
                              not more than three
marm the longitude and fortitude of the indigenous studitude
particles marm, have we discussed particles   there are 17,000
in an article
particles marm particles   we just did a recount   there are 17,000
and 50 more
                              well open a new chapter sunday
marm im going to have a new dictionary of communalests
                              dont print it down
how many regular people marm
if you cant use your mind marm you could just sort of relax
and lie back   can we charge a quarter
ma please what is noblesse oblige
                              its the obligation of those who dont to
those who
WHAT marm
suppose i raised the level of consciousness .07%
i think i can project years into the future
ma i ceded the vision center
marm we dont pray almighty myself
algosha hanoshe is a nice name   did you ever buy a purse from
his department store window
                              well id say i would carry one if i were
hitting the cavalcade
marm we dont shop even in ecstasy
poor marm   is that ok
a two penny opera   is that a good thing to think about
a cheaper one
                              definitely absolute
class consciousness marm   which comes first   the literary
class or the vermont distillery
the community collective collateral dollar   which department
do i put that in

a healer marm   what is a wheeler dealer
                                    local association   president
marm the last word
                                    very well   clerical error
ma shes teasing
suppose i was severed from my job would i get severance pay
marm i work even in my sleep
                                    well i would say he must be a wisdom
healer   very well
let us visit and bring the stuff
what kind of wisdom marm   the astral kind of the binocular
close up kind
                                    now severance pay is what we should
discuss
ma how many years can you get it
                                    well were dead already   keeps going on
                                    well i should end it with hymph
                                    very well hyrmph

pshaw
/.

                        well should sign it im an old anarchist
                        and hes a young indian   polar bear marm
                        my name marm   paw   well noa kle should be
                        received

magnum p.i.: this section is dedicated to our honest
typewriter
higgins: i daresay i should not reply
marm where is my introminium speech   maw im
applauded everywhere when i give my introminium
speech   ma please my instructions are to write down
certain words to introducimous introdification   whos
henry maw   henry is the guard paw
magnum: higgins higgins listen higgins we may just
sneak in
magnum: courtesy you know   higgins higgins we
can begin again
higgins: it has been updated prematurely
ma please preponderoneranerousimous
ma is this a good program to snoogle up with
marm please epidermescrum   i guess that cancels that
page   nevermoramousastrous
no marm thats a consideration effectiveness
i didnt get a chance   maw say simple   breviousi-
mous
maw please dont listen if im terresillimous   maw im
learning   im studying to be a great big novelermist
maw i changed it i want to be a poetastermous
ma you dont discuss tergemous
there are six of us   we had already planned a great
big wedding maw   terrillified   grass all over you
i presume
higgins: a harrowing was had by all at the recollection
brouhaha maw   tattered and torn   shluph   ma
please   orgasms and writing a literary quarterly
a pamphlet for everyone   side saddle bag   street
sale
obligatory demand   very successful enterprise maw

maw the wedding please   i was received by all of them
duplicideuteronomous
the bible heck
ma who said the line two above
osbmit   no ma we dont submit we just print   you
are
giving prose line away   maw please there are
six pairs of print color stockings where shall i hang
them   studer   maw please it isnt like that really
at least after the first four or five hours or days
paw please a circlet of lily of the valley whos wearing it
i am maw
well dear at least we know who the bridegroom is
ma please im entirely wearilimous   no ma im shocked
higgins: somewhat tired   maw thats all of us   i lay
my head down on the immediate and suffered malcrose
who ma   ma please the wedding   thanks for the
cheese and crackers
several saliva wedding tests have to be made   ma am i
still drooling
magnum: no wonder hes getting married   free love
circle and all that
the stockings are hung
serve pizza ma   peter do you want to eat   no im
astral   face reality
maw he doesnt pretenderamermous   the defense of
the illoteriate
maw there were some other desultory idiosyncrasies
higgins: i said go back   james would start a new
book right away drumperfumferfroun
ma six people at one wedding are a little hard to manage
tersipashicouse   ma cheat   tushimushimush
the wedding bra is that a necessity   black lace
hrumph
ma someone is spoiling this scenario   can we borrow
your lily white scurirmous   terserlamenanissamisse-

mous persedfluisdgrouseinhismotor   ma are we hiring
a car
i love you
i will always too   ma bullshit teredimousflousgamer-
stran
ma some people fall out of love in two days   ma who is
printing the little letters
maw bliss does it come before the wedding night during
it
or after the wedding ma   its almost a celestial happen-
ing   write it down im very happy   paw how many
girls are there   only four or five   remember six in
the party   maw they took your white lace bra and are
printing on your face anyone can attend maw   very
well
we should make a list
no maw please not another   urglemush
ma we took the black lace one too   er delusions of
virility virginity and plausible clause
ma please virginity i dont want an unused   too many
complaints   hrumph grumph i am not mentioned
dont tease her ma put her name in noa   a visitation
from abroad
no ma all are welcome   please face the hardships of a
full livingroom   terrillimous   ma im really a very
happy woman when i live downtown with you   well
dear it just sucks that paw is flurilous   no maw im
embarrassed   ma quick its a hazelnut story
write everything down was down with fidel castro
imagine ma a limousine car at the plane for me alone
higgins: a more thing   a vast irresponsible
no maw if i use only adjectives no one can tell the truth
maw please a limousine car for myself would fit seven
turpitude   close quarters ma   ma im pleased to
death your litergerminus   maw the wedding shall i
postpone it because of the castro infidel   im almost a

millionaire when i come back maw   cuban cigars are a
ration item   maw please dont over react if i come
back poor   i may give it all back to the people   maw
please we really have a narrative or a movie script and i
wrote it myself   scurriflusisstorm   selfsame   maw
who put in that end word   well we have hit the bottom
ma   castro definitely doesnt believe in wedding par-
ties   urmph grumph   too strict for infidels   please
maw im almost detained at the port illegal cigar holding
even if i clipped the ends off as if they were my own
well maw if the ship sails should i be on it   ma the agi-
tators do
they drink like everyone else   urgurgleursurlemous
maw please the cigar box they give you when you leave
has only one cigar in it per person for me   they like
suchimous maw to make you feel good   where can i
buy some for the wedding party   paw at the corner
store little ones   maw the inference is treachermous
please remember im scurimous wearisome   who used
a real word to describe maw   we didnt plan to have
such a large wedding party maw but there are 14 bride-
groom alternates   maw whats an alternate   someone
to drive the bride away
figure it out maw we are all bonded in wedded bliss
already
well dear if i were getting married i would be in a tither
and a tather and paw is flirting with two new girls
tomorrow or terrillimous   sign terrillimous
signing off paw   well the wedding party is in the living
room
pshaw

popularize popular books handling excitement abroad culture understanding knowledge in our history obvious power embarrassment knowledge thinking structure popular books under control when understanding power when handling silence power complete throughout civilization power secret acknowledges corrupt public when make it history confident overpopularize apologize without history understanding complete power analysis his silence provides commitment allowance confident power history acknowledges complaints needed understanding complete power history make complete story complete understand hurts apologize two books allowance he hurts apologize provided control without excellent sorry when obvious culture is contentment embarrassment embarrassment history apologize without spiritual understanding history polite embarrassment political without spritual knowledge understand power understand mental complete power destroy spiritual teaching without understand complete his understanding spritual understand mental sorry by structure history correct understand without knowledge understanding its sorry understanding complete silence regards history power silences understanding alone power employs understanding english culture history make culture sorry history hurts obvious sometimes obvious hurts when culture knowledges complete understanding power omits structure provided complete you silenced complains structure history off analysis congratulations hurry abroad england controls its population understand forgiven without understanding completing knowledge provided unless completing power history completing embarrassment knowledge converted history culture make unhappy content publicize public he hurts when in culture understand hurting analysis power understand controls he power conflicts understand correct spiritual obvious needed complaints when hurting philosophy granted obvious hints structure obvious handling culture history make it understanding teaching complete his understanding conflicts obvious history structure behavior cheap provided handle literature in friendly culture that it handle make handling structure knowledge understanding teaching make trouble handling spiritual understanding power controls without understanding completing knowledge pages conflict destroy power understanding completes power spiritual many power complaints when our culture provides hints allowance understand popular understanding culture without understand allowance power understanding culture allowance understand complaints when our teaching power complaints power handling civilization power understanding completing analysis without office control analysis control public offices without mental excitement.

—CLAIRVOYANTLY WRITTEN / SILENT TEACHER

PREVIOUSLY PUBLISHED BOOKS BY HANNAH WEINER
in order of composition

Magritte Poems (Poetry Newsletter, 1970)

The Code Poems (Open Studio, 1982)

The Fast (United Artists, 1992)

Country Girl (Kenning Editions, 2004)

The Early and Clairvoyant Journals (UCSD Archive for New Poetry, 2004)

Clairvoyant Journal (Angel Hair, 1978)

Little Books / Indians (Roof, 1980)

Nijole's House (Potes & Poets, 1981)

Spoke (Sun and Moon, 1984)

Sixteen (Awede, 1983)

Written In / The Zero One (Post-Neo, 1985)

Weeks (Xexoxial, 1990)

Silent Teachers / Remembered Sequel (Tender Buttons, 1993)

Page (Roof, 2002)

We Speak Silent (Roof, 1997)